SOUP, SALAD & PASTA

Bon Appétit

bouillon

3 half chicken breasts

bay leaf

thyme

Bon Appétit

SOUP, SALAD & PASTA

A collection of recipes
by Ursel Norman
Designed and illustrated by Derek Norman

GALLERY BOOKS

Contents

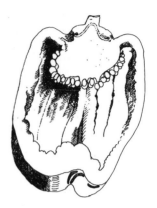

GALLERY BOOKS
An Imprint of W. H. Smith Publishers Inc.
112 Madison Avenue
New York City 10016

Manufactured in Spain
Printed by Graficromo, S.A.

2 3 4 5 6 7 8 9 10

ISBN 0–8317–7916–0

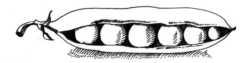

SOUP CONTENTS

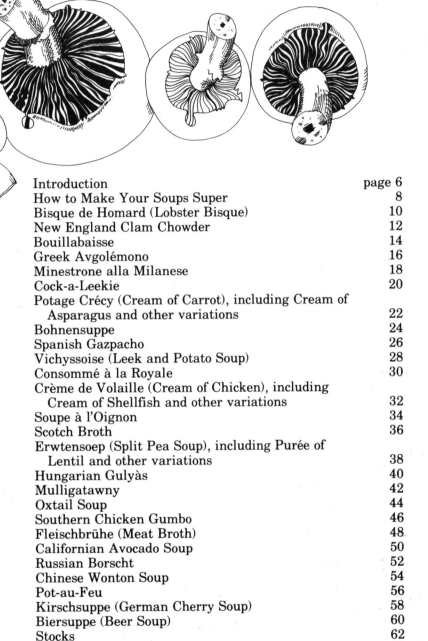

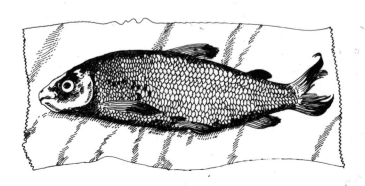

INTRODUCTION

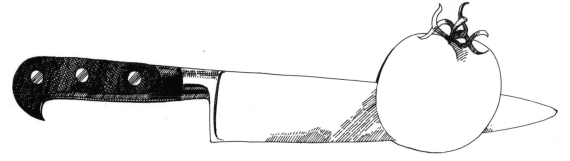

Beautiful Soup! Who cares for fish,
Game, or any other dish?
Who would not give all else for two
pennyworth only of beautiful Soup?
Beau-ootiful Soup!
Beau-ootiful Soup!
Soo-oop of the e-e-evening,
Beautiful, beauti-FUL Soup!

This famed piece from *Alice in Wonderland* by Lewis Carroll is but a taste of the wealth of poetic language that has helped immortalize soup. For centuries soup has given inspiration to peasants and poets and sent gourmets into lyrical raptures. For soup is a dish to stimulate the imagination and whet the appetite. As one early 20th century gourmet put it: 'There is nothing like a plate of hot soup, its wisp of aromatic steam making the nostrils quiver with anticipation . . . one whiff of a savoury, aromatic soup and appetites come to attention.'
Soup has historically played a highly significant part in man's existence, for it was a basis for nourishment and survival. The cauldron was the original stock-pot and provided an ever changing broth enriched daily with whatever ingredients happened to be available.
Such simple peasant fare gave birth to the earliest of the myriad national soups, many of which fortunately survive. For every country, there is virtually a national soup. Their preparation is often somewhat similar, but differing by virtue of ingredients, which reflect regional and national tastes. Some of the most famous are Pot-au-Feu from France, Minestrone from Italy, Borscht from Russia, Gazpacho from Spain and Erwtensoep from Holland.
Within this book you will find all of these soups, together with many more, each with its classic flavor representing some of the finest of European and American cookery. All have their individual tastes, aromas and rich historical associations. Their different characteristics reflect the gastronomic cultures from which they originate, tastes never to be found in any can, but easily and inexpensively produced within any home kitchen.

Escoffier in his famous *Guide Culinaire* divides soups into two leading classes. 1) 'Clear soups, which include plain and garnished consommés. 2) Thick soups, which comprise the Purées, Veloutés and Creams.' The first class are clear meat or poultry broths, frequently served with some kind of dainty garnish. The second class of soups are made with some kind of starchy ingredient, producing cream soups of various kinds. There is a third type of soup, usually a main-dish soup, like, for instance, Erwtensoep, Minestrone or Gumbo, which are very popular. These fall somewhere in between the first two categories. There are many examples of all three categories within the pages of *Soup, Beautiful Soup*.

It is our sincere hope that the reader will be inspired to make extensive use of the recipes within these pages and that the very thought of homemade soup will send the cook scuttling into the kitchen!

We trust that both the style and content of this book do more than justice to the subject of soups and that the 'Look and Cook' format will prove a useful and practical tool in the kitchen. For it is designed so that the reader can comprehend at a glance how a dish is prepared and how it should look when finally it reaches the table.

Finally, we owe a debt of gratitude and thanks to all our tasters, on both sides of the Atlantic, who have kindly helped us appraise the taste and quality of all the recipes in this book. We hope the reader will find them as tantalizing as we do, proving to be feasts for your eye as well as your palate! For what can be better, or bettered, than:

'Soo-oop of the e-e-evening,
Beautiful, beauti-FUL Soup!'

HOW TO MAKE YOUR SOUPS SUPER

Some Do's and Don'ts

Stocks

Almost all the recipes in this book use stock as the cooking liquid. Only when a large amount of meat and bone is used will water do. The best stocks, of course, are the ones you make yourself (recipes page 62). And if you have the time, do try them. The soup can only be as good as the ingredients that you put in – a good stock is half the battle.

However, canned stocks or bouillon cubes can be substituted as long as you remember that the latter are usually highly seasoned. So go carefully on other seasoning, salt especially.

Skimming

Most soups throw up a lot of frothy scum just before they come to a boil. This ought to be skimmed off as best you can. It helps to give the soup a fresh, clear, clean taste and color.

The best skimming tool is a soup ladle. Dip the ladle in a basin of cold water, shake dry, then dip it straight down into the soup (or stock) but *only just* below the surface, and skim off any froth that accumulates at the sides of the pot. Rinse the ladle in the basin with cold water before repeating the process. Further scum will also be thrown against the sides of the pot, so keep skimming just the sides. Skim and rinse until the scum ceases to appear.

Degreasing

Degreasing is done in much the same way as skimming. Only when there is little fat left on the surface, and skimming gets too difficult, can you use a spoon to lift off the remaining "eyes". If you have trouble getting them out, run a paper towel across the surface quickly to mop up some of the grease. No soup – indeed no food – should ever appear on the table with a film of fat on it. One easy way to get it off is to let the soup get cold in the refrigerator. The cold will harden the fat on the surface and you can lift it off easily.

Soup meats

The best meats for soups are those with bones, whether beef, lamb or chicken. These are usually the most inexpensive ones too, and they don't suffer from the long cooking.

Soup Vegetables

Many, many vegetables are used in soup making. But apart from those which give the soup its name and taste, there are the "aromatic" vegetables that appear in almost all soups: onions, carrots and celery. Their flavor is greatly enhanced if they are sautéed in a little butter or margarine before being added.

Soup Pots

A good soup pot is a large, heavy-bottomed aluminium pot with a lid, rather taller than wide, of about a 20-pint (10 quart) capacity. A thin, light aluminium pot with a thin bottom and sides is unsuitable, since it is bound to burn the longer-cooking soups.

If you do not possess such a pot – and they are not cheap – do invest in one. You'll find lots of other uses for it, like cooking pasta or large amounts of greens, corn-on-the-cob, etc.

Covering the Pot

Very frequently in this book you will find the term "partially covered." This means that the lid should be set askew *just* a little, leaving only a tiny crack open. The escape of moisture will be minimal, since most of it will accumulate on the underside of the lid and drop back into the pot. The reason for doing this is to stop the soup from boiling too rapidly – and to stop the lid from rattling. If "uncovered" is mentioned, this is done to concentrate the flavors through evaporation.

Straining

A variety of soups need straining at some point, either to remove certain ingredients or to be made absolutely smooth.

In most cases the use of a fine-mesh strainer is sufficient. If a soup is too thick to pass through, use the back of a soup ladle to push it through. Far easier than stirring it around with a spoon.

In the case of clear broths or consommés, it is necessary to line the strainer with a damp cloth (wrung out in *cold* water). This dampening expands the fibres of the cloth to make it more efficient. This way even the smallest particles are held back.

Good straining cloths are cotton (not synthetic) that are easy to wash and keep clean. (Top of the list are cloth diapers!)

Thickeners

Many soups contain some amount of starchy thickeners. This can be flour, cornflour, rice or other cereal or potatoes. These are all neutral in taste and color.

Puréed soups made from starchy vegetables (peas or beans) contain enough starch already and don't need thickeners.

Use of the Electric Blender

By far the most efficient way of using a blender is with the lid off. This of course is not practical all the time, especially when small children are trying to get a peep at what is going on, but when all is quiet and peaceful, use this method:

With the motor in the off position, pour one soup-ladleful into the blender jar. Turn the blender to the lowest speed. When the contents are smooth, add a second ladleful, then a third. When all this is smooth, turn to the highest speed and keep it there for a minute or two, or until the soup is absolutely smooth. Never do more than 3 ladlefuls at a time; over-filling reduces the efficiency.

If the soup is too thick to be puréed, thin it down with a little of whatever cooking liquid was used in the recipe (stock).

Flavor Enhancers and Food Color

Absolutely none, ever, in anything! Food colors are quite unnecessary anyway. No food needs to look more yellow or more green than nature made it, and correct seasoning eliminate any need for flavor enhancers.

Freezing Soups

Nearly all soups can be frozen without any loss of taste or texture. If it does look lumpy after defrosting, a quick beating with a wire whisk during reheating will restore the smoothness. Guides to which soups can be frozen are included in the recipes.

1 pound of raw lobster meat,
  fresh or frozen, cut into
  ½-inch chunks
1 medium carrot, chopped
1 medium onion, chopped
2 parsley stalks, chopped
6 tbsp. butter
½ tsp. dried thyme
1 bayleaf
2 tbsp. brandy
½ cup white wine
2 pints chicken stock or
  bouillon
⅜ cup long grain rice,
  uncooked
1 pint water
4 tbsp. unsalted butter
¼ cup heavy cream
cayenne pepper to taste
salt and pepper to taste
Serves 5–6

1   In the soup pot, sauté the chopped onion, carrot and parsley in the butter for 5 minutes. Add the thyme and bayleaf and sauté further until the vegetables just begin to brown.

3   Pour the brandy into a small soup ladle and ignite it by holding it over a gas flame (or use a match). When the brandy is actually burning, pour it over the fish and the vegetables, shaking the pot vigorously until the flame dies down.

4   Then add the wine. Boil the mixture over a high heat until the liquid has reduced to less than half.

5   Add the stock and simmer the bisque, uncovered, for about 10 minutes.

6   Meanwhile, boil the rice in the water till tender (about 20 minutes). Add the rice and water to the soup.

7   Purée the soup in the blender until it is absolutely smooth, first on low speed for a minute, then on high. Strain it through a fine-mesh strainer, pushing it down with the back of a soup ladle. Discard what does not go through. Return soup to pot.

8   Bring the soup to a boil and skim as necessary. Also skim off any fat that rises to the surface. Boil it, uncovered, until the scum no longer appears.

Just before serving, blend in the butter and cream and season to taste with cayenne, salt and pepper.

Note For Bisque de Crevettes (Shrimp Bisque) substitute 1 pound of shelled shrimp for the lobster meat. (Shrimp will need to be cooked an extra 5–10 minutes at stage 5.) For bisque de Crabe (Crabmeat Bisque) substitute 1 pound of crabmeat for the lobster meat.

Bisque can be made ahead up to stage 7, and even frozen if necessary.

Brandy

Flame

BUTTER

chopped onion

thyme

bayleaf

ine

stock

COOKED RICE
& COOKING WATER

return to pot

Strain

LOBSTER MEAT

2   Add the chunks of lobster meat and stir them around with the vegetables until the lobster acquires a nice pink color.

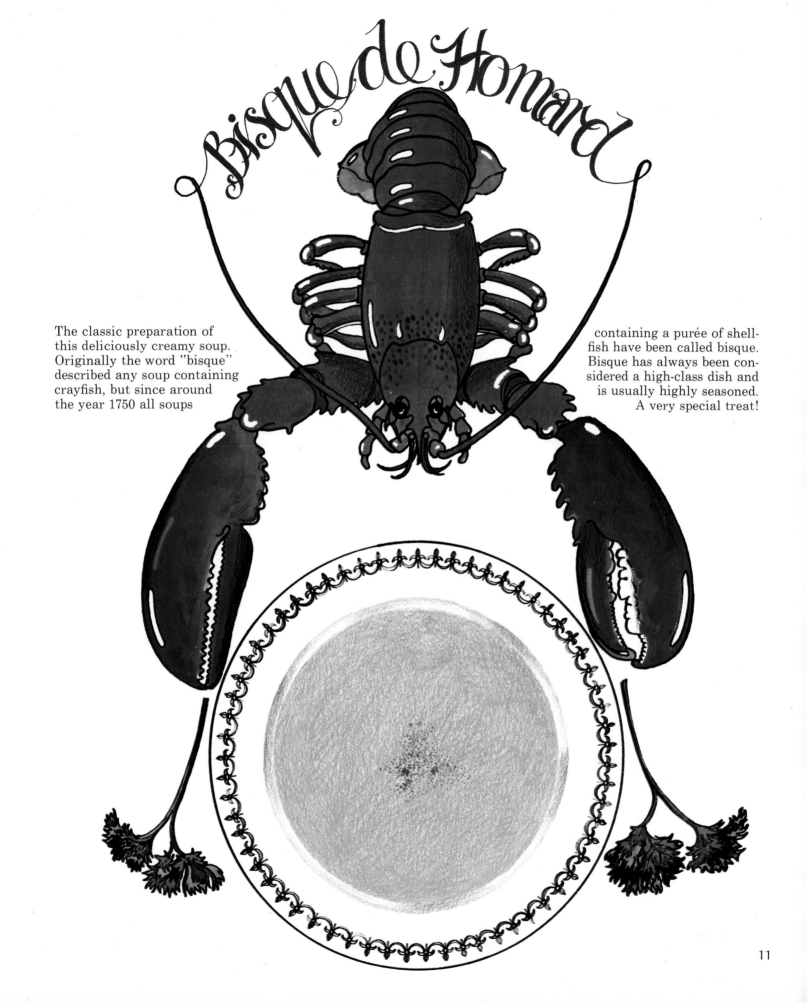

Bisque de Homard

The classic preparation of this deliciously creamy soup. Originally the word "bisque" described any soup containing crayfish, but since around the year 1750 all soups containing a purée of shellfish have been called bisque. Bisque has always been considered a high-class dish and is usually highly seasoned. A very special treat!

2 oz. salt pork *or* fat bacon, diced very fine
2 medium onions, finely chopped
3 medium potatoes, diced
½ tsp. dried thyme
1 pint clam juice or water
3 cans (6½ oz. each) minced clams and their liquid *or* 2 dozen finely chopped raw clams and all their liquid plus 1 pint clam juice or water

1 pint rich milk *or* half-and-half)
5 tbsp. flour
salt and pepper to taste
finely chopped parsley for garnish
a little paprika for garnish

Serves 6–7

3 Now add the minced or fresh clams and their liquid, and the milk or half-and-half. Simmer, uncovered, about 10 minutes.

4 Mix the flour with enough water to make a pouring consistency. Pour into the boiling soup slowly, stirring all the time with a wire whisk. Simmer, stirring all the time, for 3 minutes. Season to taste with salt and pepper.

Sprinkle with chopped parsley and a dusting of paprika. Traditionally served with crackers.

Note Reheats, but does not freeze.

SALT PORK

finely chopped

CLAM JUICE

Milk

thyme

3 potatoes peeled & diced

Flour

water

season to taste

1 In a large saucepan set over medium heat sauté the salt pork or bacon until it has rendered all its fat and is lightly browned. Add the onions and sauté the mixture until the onions are soft and transparent.

2 Add the potatoes, thyme and clam juice or water, and simmer, uncovered, until the potatoes are cooked but not falling apart.

NEW ENGLAND CLAM CHOWDER

The name chowder is derived from the French *chaudière* (literally meaning the fish kettle in which the dish was cooked) and was probably anglicized subsequent to the French settling in Canada. New England Clam Chowder is by far the most distinguished of all the clam chowders, with its characteristic clams, salt pork and milk or cream. Herman Melville immortalized the dish in his salty classic, *Moby Dick*. 'Oh! sweet friends, harken to me. It was made of small juicy clams, scarcely bigger than hazelnuts, mixed with pounded ships biscuits, and salted pork cut up into little flakes, the whole enriched with butter and plentifully seasoned with pepper and salt.' The recipe here you will find a little more reliable, though guaranteed to rouse similar feelings of delight. We feel sure Herman Melville would have approved.

2 pounds fresh tomatoes,
   peeled and chopped, *or* one
   2-pound can tomatoes,
   chopped
2 large onions, chopped
4–8 cloves garlic, crushed
2 sprigs parsley
1 bayleaf
1 tsp. dried thyme
4–5 fennel seeds
2 pinches saffron
1 fresh or frozen lobster tail
   (shell left on and cut
   vertically into 2-inch slices)
3 pounds various firm fish, cut
   into serving pieces (leaving
   the skin on some adds color).
   Choose from: halibut, pike,
   cod, haddock or red snapper
1 cup olive oil
1 tsp. pepper
2 tsp. salt

11 cups liquid, either cold
   water *or* ⅔ water and ⅓ white
   wine *or* fish stock from page
   62
3 pounds various soft fish, cut
   into serving pieces (leave the
   skin on some). Choose from:
   mackerel, whiting, whitefish,
   flounder, sole, mullet or
   perch
12 croûtons (optional). These
   are slices of French bread,
   brushed with oil on both
   sides and toasted in a 325°
   oven till crisp and dry

Serves 10–12

1 Place the tomatoes, their juice,
   onion, garlic, parsley, bayleaf,
   thyme, fennel seeds and saffron
   into large soup pot.

2 On the bed of vegetables and
   herbs place the cut up lobster
   tail and all the pieces of firm
   fish. Pour over this the olive oil,
   1 teaspoon pepper and 2
   teaspoons salt.

3 Cover the fish and vegetables
   with the liquid. Bring to a boil
   over very high heat. Continue
   boiling rapidly (do *not* turn down
   the heat), uncovered, for 7–8
   minutes.

LOBSTER TAIL

FIRM FISH

fennelseeds

salt

thyme

wine
optional

SOFT FISH

water & wine
(or fish stock)

4 Now add all the soft fish.
   Continue boiling on high heat
   another 7 minutes. Taste for
   seasoning.

5 To serve: Using a slotted spoon,
   transfer all the fish to a platter.
   Serve the broth in deep soup
   plates. Pass the fish separately.
   (If croûtons are used, place one
   in each soup plate first, then
   spoon the broth on top, then the
   fish.)

Note *Do not freeze!* This soup can be
reheated – with a minimum of stirring
so as not to break up the fish.

BOUILLABAISSE

In his poem 'The Ballad of Bouillabaisse,' William Thackery has helped immortalize this hearty Mediterranean dish. Bouillabaisse is generally recognized as having originated in Marseilles, although many areas in Provence claim to make the genuine Bouillabaisse. Try this Marseillaise Bouillabaisse, great with good company and hearty conversation. The Parisian version would also include mussels or clams. A rich spicy main-dish soup.

5 cups rich chicken stock or bouillon
¼ cup long-grain rice, uncooked
2 whole eggs *or* **1 egg and 2 egg yolks**
juice of 1 lemon
a little salt (if needed)

Serves 4–5

1 Heat the chicken stock to boiling point. Slowly stir in the rice and simmer, partially covered, until the rice is tender (15–20 minutes).

3 With a wire whisk stir this mixture into the soup, and stirring constantly let it only *just* come to a boil. Remove from heat immediately.

Season with salt if necessary.

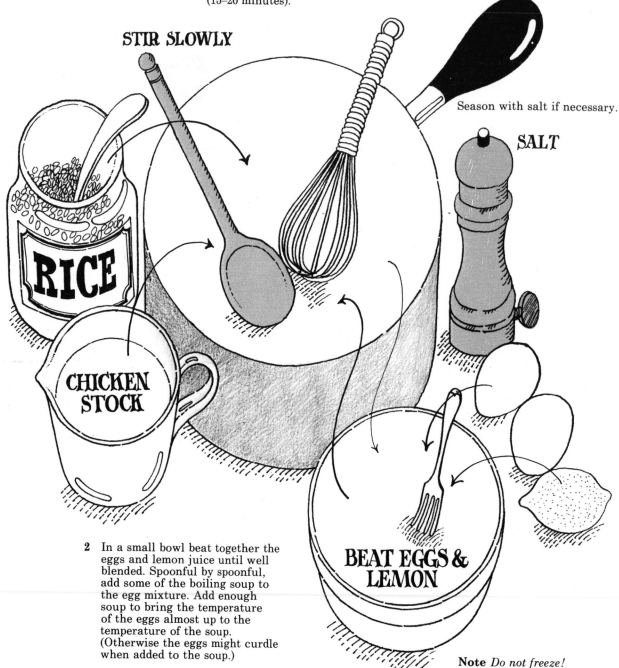

STIR SLOWLY

RICE

CHICKEN STOCK

SALT

BEAT EGGS & LEMON

2 In a small bowl beat together the eggs and lemon juice until well blended. Spoonful by spoonful, add some of the boiling soup to the egg mixture. Add enough soup to bring the temperature of the eggs almost up to the temperature of the soup. (Otherwise the eggs might curdle when added to the soup.)

Note *Do not freeze!*

GREEK AUGOLÉMONO

The best known of Greek soups. Simple ingredients are combined to create a fragrant tangy flavor.

½ pound dry white beans, washed
5 tbsp. oil
1 large onion, cut into neat cubes
1 stalk celery, cut into neat cubes
2 or more cloves garlic, crushed
3 medium carrots, cut into neat cubes
8 oz. fresh or frozen peas
½ pound unpeeled zucchini
   (cut into neat cubes)
2 leeks, chopped (if available)
½ pound cabbage, shredded
½ tsp. dried rosemary
2 oz. salt pork *or* streaky bacon, cubed
1 pound fresh tomatoes, peeled and
   chopped *or* one 16-oz. can tomatoes,
   roughly chopped

4 pints beef stock or bouillon
1 bayleaf
2 parsley sprigs } **tied together**
salt and pepper to taste
½ cup uncooked rice *or* 4 oz. soup
   noodles
5 tbsp. grated parmesan cheese

4 Sauté the diced salt pork or
bacon in the same frying
pan till crisp and brown.
Drain on paper towel and
reserve.

Serves 10

Sauté until crisp & brown

salt pork

drain

1 Soak the
beans
overnight
in
enough
water
to
cover.

2 Cook the beans,
covered, in the soaking
water until tender, about
1–1½ hours. Add a little more
water if they become too dry.
Drain and reserve.

drain

5 Into a large pot place the sautéed vegetables. Stir
in the tomatoes, beef stock, bayleaf and parsley.
Bring to a boil and simmer, partially covered, for
about 20 minutes.

3 Meanwhile,
heat the oil
in a heavy frying pan. In it sauté the onion,
celery, garlic, carrot, fresh peas (if peas are
frozen, add them later), zucchini, leeks and
cabbage. Sauté them, stirring often, for 10
minutes. Stir in the rosemary.
Remove from pan and reserve.

SAUTÉ

oil

stock

skinned &
chopped

ROSEMARY

6 Add the rice or noodles, reserved
beans and pork, and the peas (if
frozen). Simmer, partially
covered, 15–20 minutes longer. Discard
bayleaf and parsley. Taste for seasoning.

Pass the grated parmesan
separately.

Note Reheats and freezes
well.

Minestrone alla Milanese

An Italian classic with numerous regional variations. This particular recipe is a typical Milanese version, using rice as the thickener. Minestrone is to Italy what Pot au Feu is to France – it contains all the natural goodness and nutrition of fresh vegetables to give a hearty main-dish soup.

1 Cover the leeks with cold water and sprinkle some salt over them. Leave to soak for 20 minutes or so. Rinse well; leeks are usually very sandy.

1½ pounds fresh leeks, sliced ¼-inch thick
about 2 tsp. salt
1 small chicken
3 cups chicken stock or bouillon
3 parsley sprigs ⎱ tied together
1 bay leaf ⎰
½ tsp. dried thyme
⅓ cup pearl barley
1 cup heavy cream (or to taste)
salt and pepper to taste
chopped parsley for garnish

Serves 4

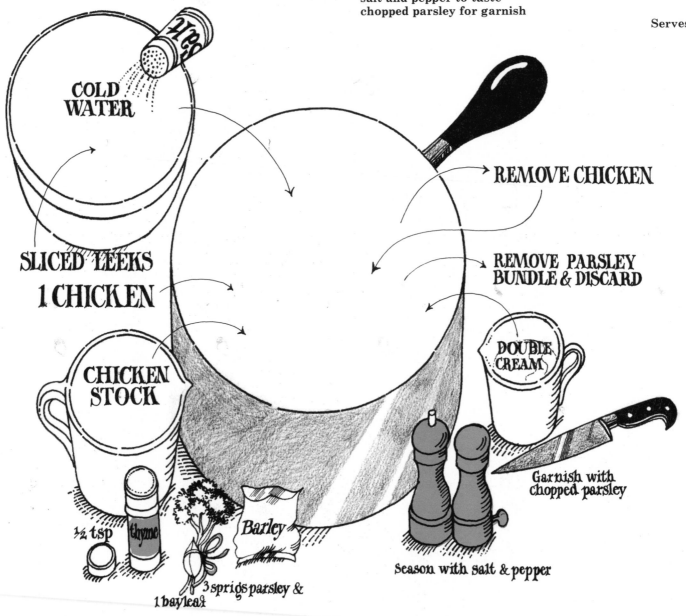

COLD WATER

SLICED LEEKS
1 CHICKEN

CHICKEN STOCK

½ tsp   thyme

Barley

3 sprigs parsley &
1 bay leaf

REMOVE CHICKEN

REMOVE PARSLEY BUNDLE & DISCARD

DOUBLE CREAM

Garnish with chopped parsley

Season with salt & pepper

2 Put the chicken into a large soup pot. Add the stock or bouillon, parsley/bayleaf bundle, thyme and barley. Simmer the soup, partially covered, for about 40 minutes. Then add the sliced leeks and cook another 15 minutes or so, until the barley is tender.

3 Remove the chicken and reserve. Lift out the parsley bundle and discard. When cool enough to handle, skin and bone the chicken carefully and cut the meat into bite-size pieces. Return meat to soup pot and heat through again.

4 Off the heat, stir in the cream, and season well with salt and pepper. Reheat to just below boiling point. Garnish with chopped parsley.

Note This soup can be made ahead of time and reheated (or frozen) up to stage 3.
(If liked, the soup can be bound with a little cornstarch and water mixture at stage 4.)

COCK~A~LEEKIE

As the name suggests, this soup was originally made with a cockerel. Nowadays a chicken is more than an adequate substitute. A hearty main-dish soup – absolutely delight-ful on a cold winter's day, with good conversation and warm, crusty bread.

See! the smoking bowl before us,
Mark our jovial ragged ring!
Round and round take up the chorus,
And in raptures let us sing.
R. Burns

Potage Crécy (*Cream of Carrot*)
1 pound carrots, roughly chopped
1 large onion, roughly chopped
2 tbsp. butter or margarine
2½ cups chicken stock or bouillon
1 oz. raw rice
salt and pepper to taste
1 egg yolk
¾ cup light cream (*or* **half-and-half**)
chopped parsley *or* **chives for**
  garnish   **Serves 4**

3 Put soup into blender jar and purée on low speed for a minute. Then turn to high speed until the soup is really smooth. (If the soup should be too thick for puréeing, add a little extra stock.) Strain through a fine-mesh strainer.

4 Return to pot and bring back to boil. Mix egg yolk into the cream and, stirring briskly with a wire whisk, stir it into the soup. Let it bubble up once or twice, then remove from heat immediately. *Do not boil again.*

1 Sauté the chopped carrots and onion over medium heat in the butter for 5 minutes, stirring frequently.

Garnish with chopped parsley
or chives.

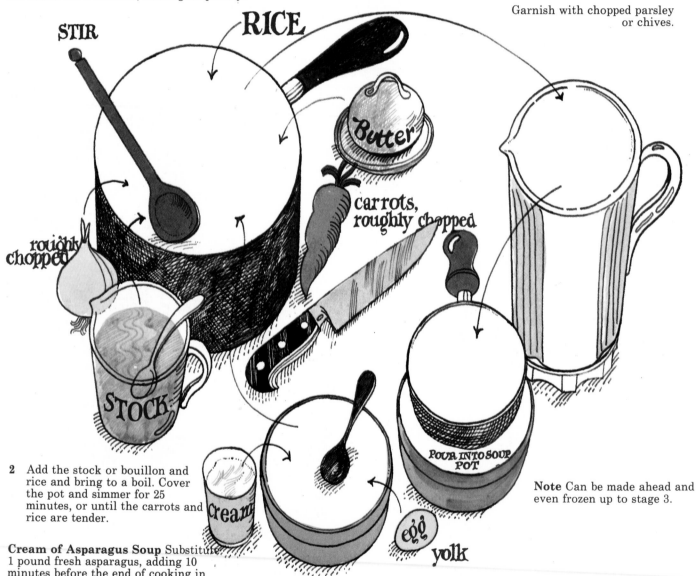

2 Add the stock or bouillon and rice and bring to a boil. Cover the pot and simmer for 25 minutes, or until the carrots and rice are tender.

Note Can be made ahead and even frozen up to stage 3.

Cream of Asparagus Soup Substitute 1 pound fresh asparagus, adding 10 minutes before the end of cooking in stage 2. (The tips can be poached separately for 5 minutes and added to the soup for garnish.)
Cream of Celery Soup Substitute 1 bunch of celery at stage 1.
Cream of Turnip Substitute 1 pound of turnips at stage 1. (Some leaves can be poached for 5 minutes and added as garnish.)
Cream of Kohlrabi Substitute 1 pound of kohlrabi at stage 1. (Some leaves can be poached for 5 minutes and added as garnish.)

Cream of Celery Root Substitute 1 cubed celery root at stage 1.
Cream of Spinach Substitute 1 pound fresh or frozen spinach leaves 10 minutes before the end of cooking time in stage 2. (Traditional garnish is hardboiled-egg slices.)
Cream of Broccoli Substitute 1 pound fresh broccoli 10 minutes before the end of cooking time in stage 2.
Cream of Cauliflower Substitute 1 pound fresh cauliflower 15 minutes

before the end of cooking time in stage 2. (A few leaves, blanched for 5 minutes, make a nice garnish.)
Cream of Fresh Peas and Lettuce Substitute 1 pound shelled peas and 1 roughly chopped head of Boston lettuce 15 minutes before end of cooking time in stage 2.
Cream of Brussels Sprouts Substitute 1 pound fresh brussels sprouts 15 minutes before the end of cooking time in stage 2.

Celery Soup
A fresh vegetable soup that can be enjoyed all year round.

Spinach Soup
A magnificent taste of spinach that would make Popeye proud! Fresh, appetizing color.

Potage Crécy
A simple, basic recipe that allows for all kinds of variations. Potage Crécy has a delightful orange color, is mildly sweet and very creamy.

Asparagus Soup
Delightful – hot *or* cold!

Kohlrabi Soup
A creamy soup, with a delicate taste and texture. Very good hot *or* cold!

1½–2 pounds beef for soup (chuck neck bones are good to add)
4 pints beef stock or bouillon
1 pound pole beans, sliced diagonally
1 large potato, peeled and cubed
1 onion, chopped
1 carrot, chopped
salt and pepper to taste

Serves 6–8

1   Place the meat in a large soup pot. Pour on the stock. Bring to a boil and skim off any scum that rises to the surface. Add onion and carrot and simmer, partially covered, for 1 hour.

2   Remove the meat and leave to cool slightly.

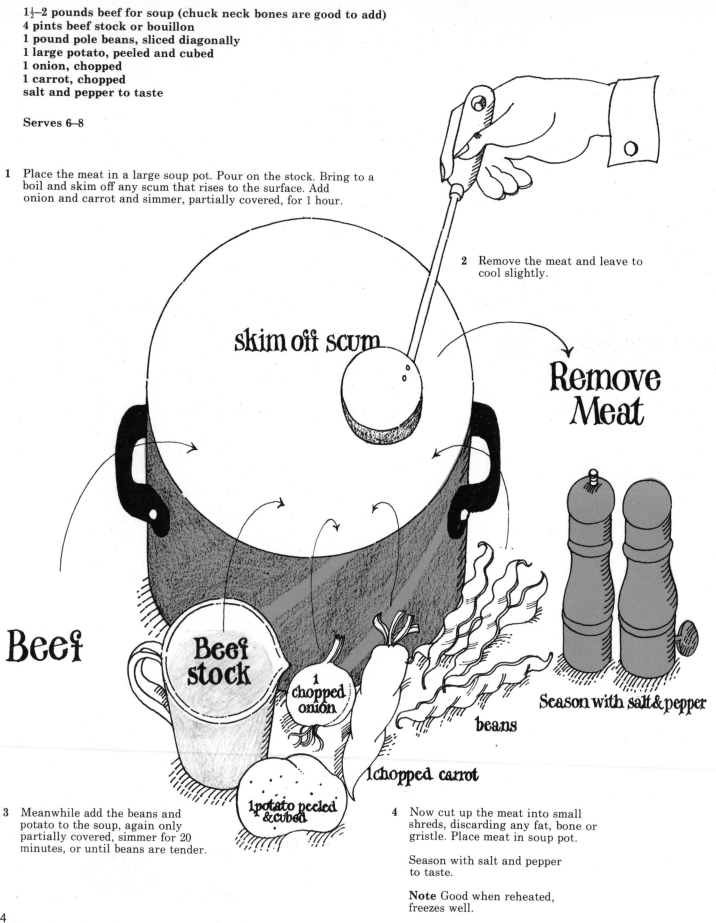

skim off scum

Remove Meat

Beef

Beef stock

1 chopped onion

beans

1 chopped carrot

1 potato peeled & cubed

Season with salt & pepper

3   Meanwhile add the beans and potato to the soup, again only partially covered, simmer for 20 minutes, or until beans are tender.

4   Now cut up the meat into small shreds, discarding any fat, bone or gristle. Place meat in soup pot.

Season with salt and pepper to taste.

Note Good when reheated, freezes well.

Bohnensuppe

A Westphalian soup that oozes a country earthiness. Honest and sincere, extremely low in calories, and full of nutrition. Serve it piping hot for a fine lunch. A meal in itself, especially with crusty bread. Guten Appetit.

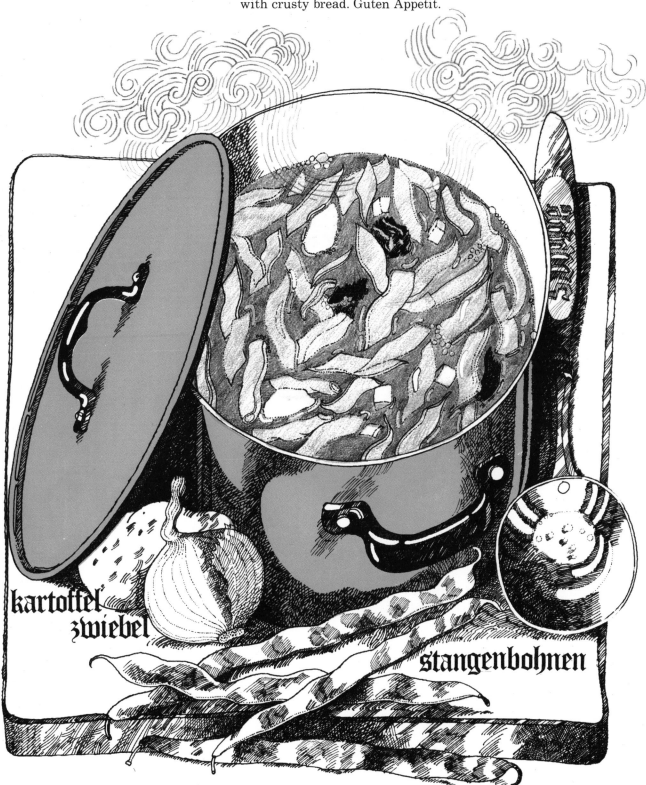

kartoffel
zwiebel

stangenbohnen

2½ pounds fresh tomatoes, peeled and chopped
1 small, peeled and chopped cucumber
1 clove garlic, crushed
1 green pepper, cut into strips
2 tbsp. tomato purée
1 large parsley sprig
¾ cup cold water
4 tbsp. oil
2 tbsp. white wine vinegar
salt and pepper to taste
2 slices ordinary white bread, crust removed, cubed
2 finely sliced green (spring) onions
1 stalk celery, very finely chopped } for garnish
a few black olives

Serves 6

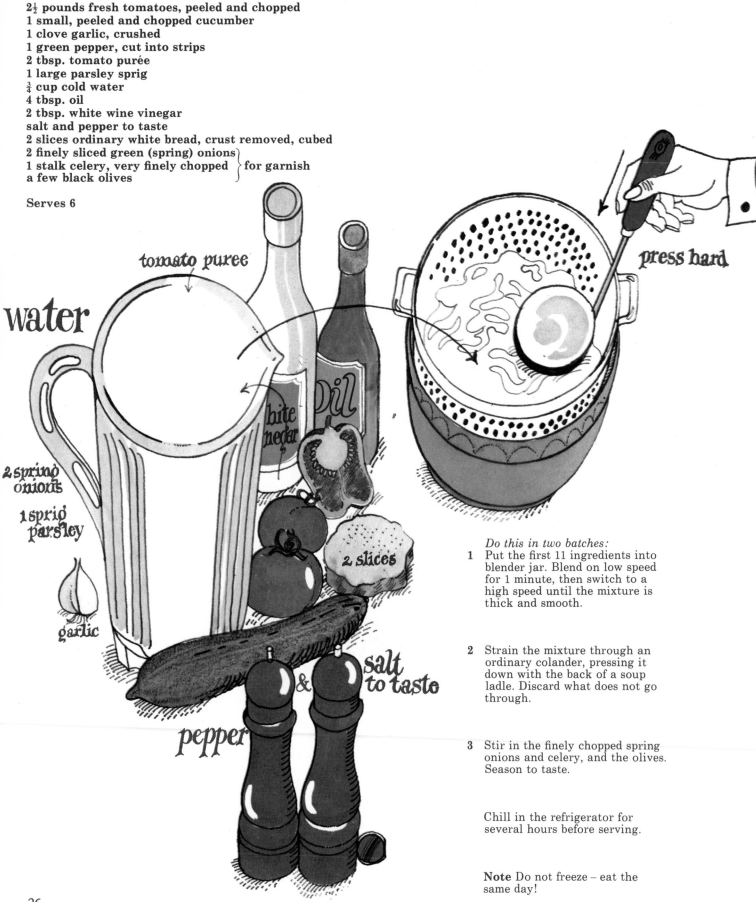

Do this in two batches:

1 Put the first 11 ingredients into blender jar. Blend on low speed for 1 minute, then switch to a high speed until the mixture is thick and smooth.

2 Strain the mixture through an ordinary colander, pressing it down with the back of a soup ladle. Discard what does not go through.

3 Stir in the finely chopped spring onions and celery, and the olives. Season to taste.

Chill in the refrigerator for several hours before serving.

Note Do not freeze – eat the same day!

SPANISH GAZPACHO

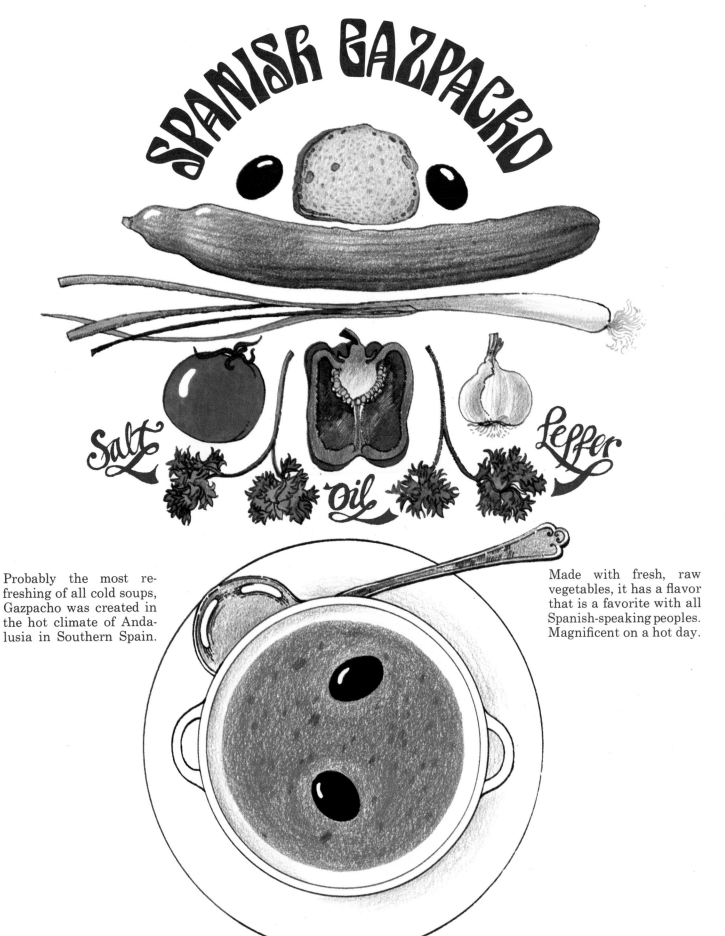

Probably the most refreshing of all cold soups, Gazpacho was created in the hot climate of Andalusia in Southern Spain.

Made with fresh, raw vegetables, it has a flavor that is a favorite with all Spanish-speaking peoples. Magnificent on a hot day.

Salt

Oil

Pepper

2 pounds leeks, white part only, sliced
½ pound raw, peeled potato, cubed
3 tbsp. butter
5 cups chicken stock or bouillon
½ cup heavy cream
salt and pepper to taste
chopped chives or parsley for garnish
Serves 5–6

1 Soak the sliced leeks in salted water for 20 minutes. Rinse and drain well.

SOAK SLICED LEEKS

DRAIN

SAUTÉ in BUTTER

Potato peeled & cubed

CHICKEN STOCK

STRAIN

CREAM

2 Sauté the leeks and potatoes in butter in a large soup pot for about 10 minutes.

3 Add the chicken stock or bouillon and simmer the soup, partially covered, for 30 minutes.

4 Put the soup into a blender and purée on low speed for 1 minute. Switch to a high speed and purée until absolutely smooth. Strain through a fine-mesh strainer.

5 Pour the soup back into the pot, reheat, and off the heat stir in the cream.

Serve hot or chilled, garnished with chives or parsley.

28

Note The soup can be made ahead and reheated or frozen up to stage 4.

Vichyssoise

Vichyssoise is a beautiful soup of fresh leeks and potatoes, and is only served cold. There is no need here to do as Edward Lear's Young Lady of Poole did,

"whose soup was excessively cool,
so she put it to boil by the aid of some oil,
That ingenious young lady of Poole!"

(If Vichyssoise is served hot, it becomes Potage Crème de Poireaux.) Vichyssoise makes a fine, elegant soup for a formal occasion. Very delicate in taste and texture. Bon Appétit!

for the consommé
5–6 egg whites
2 tsp. salt
½ tsp. pepper
4 cloves
**2 pounds very, very lean ground
  beef (the meat should be from
  an old animal; young ones yield
  very little flavor)**
1 cup red wine (optional)
8 cups beef stock

Serves 6–8

for the royale
4 parsley sprigs
little salt and pepper
**5 fl. oz. consommé or chicken
  bouillon**
1 egg
2 egg yolks

3　To the meat mixture add the cold beef stock
　　and then pour the mixture into a saucepan.

4　Bring to a boil, and simmer (uncovered) very
　　slowly for 1½ to 2 hours, *never* stirring. The
　　liquid must simmer very gently, not come
　　bubbling through the meat mixture. Cook until
　　the cake that has formed on the surface is
　　quite cooked, with no traces of red.

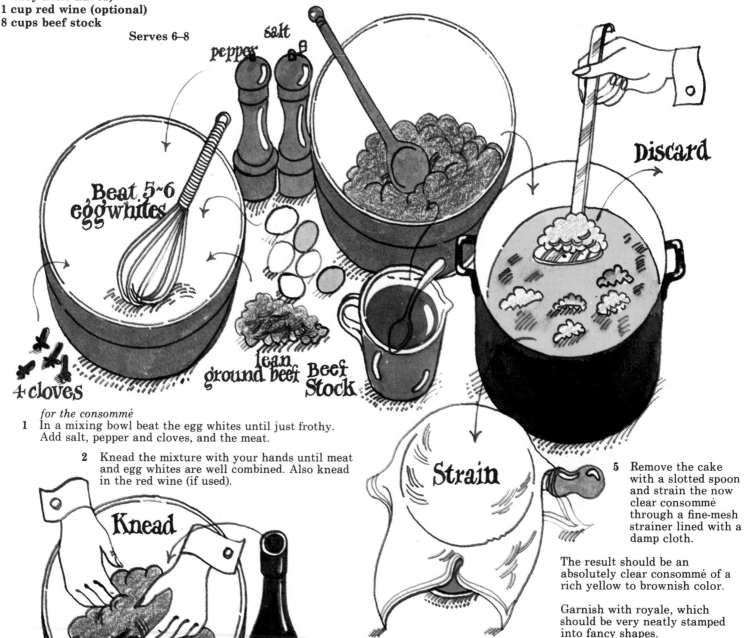

for the consommé

1　In a mixing bowl beat the egg whites until just frothy.
　　Add salt, pepper and cloves, and the meat.

2　Knead the mixture with your hands until meat
　　and egg whites are well combined. Also knead
　　in the red wine (if used).

5　Remove the cake
　　with a slotted spoon
　　and strain the now
　　clear consommé
　　through a fine-mesh
　　strainer lined with a
　　damp cloth.

The result should be an
absolutely clear consommé of a
rich yellow to brownish color.

Garnish with royale, which
should be very neatly stamped
into fancy shapes.

for the royale
Simmer the parsley, salt and pepper in the stock for 5 minutes.
Cool and remove the parsley. Beat the egg and egg yolks well
and add them to the cool stock. Strain the mixture through a
fine-mesh strainer. Pour the mixture into a buttered
ovenproof flat dish (the mixture should be about ¼ inch deep). Skim
off any foam that might form on the surface.
Fill a baking tray with boiling water and set the ovenproof dish
into it. Place in a preheated 325° oven for 20 minutes. (Test for
doneness with a knife; if it comes out clean, the royale is cooked.)
Cool in the dish before cutting.

Other garnishes for consommés
All garnishes for consommés have to be cooked separately, well drained and rinsed to keep them absolutely clean, julienned
vegetables blanched 1 minute and rinsed, rice or noodles cooked till tender and rinsed, leftover roast or boiled meat cut into
julienne strips, quenelles or profiteroles.

Consommé à la Royale

The word "consommé" literally means a perfectly refined soup. This recipe is a basic consommé, garnished with 'royale.' There are numerous variations of this recipe, each largely differentiated by the type of garnish. Escoffier lists over 70 different kinds. Consommé, it is worth remembering, represents perfection, pure and exquisite. No rustic country character here. Beautifully clear, it stimulates the appetite as no other soup can. Perfect for formal occasions. A triumph of haute cuisine. Bon Appétit.

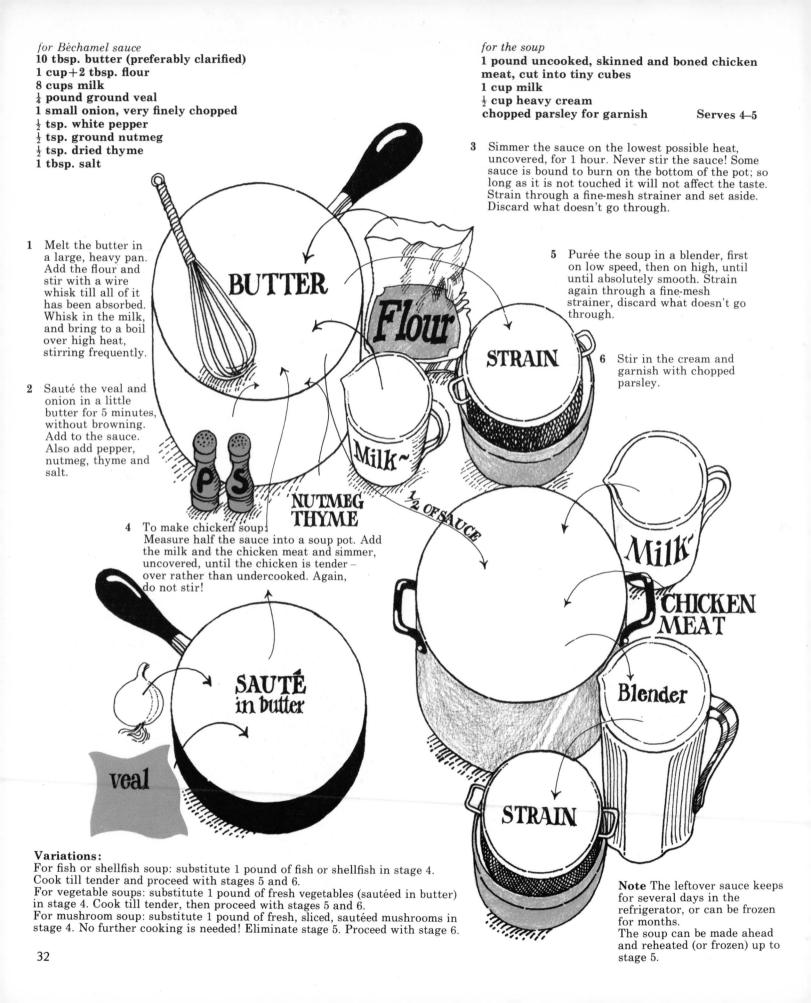

for Béchamel sauce
10 tbsp. butter (preferably clarified)
1 cup + 2 tbsp. flour
8 cups milk
¼ pound ground veal
1 small onion, very finely chopped
½ tsp. white pepper
½ tsp. ground nutmeg
½ tsp. dried thyme
1 tbsp. salt

for the soup
1 pound uncooked, skinned and boned chicken meat, cut into tiny cubes
1 cup milk
½ cup heavy cream
chopped parsley for garnish   Serves 4–5

1 Melt the butter in a large, heavy pan. Add the flour and stir with a wire whisk till all of it has been absorbed. Whisk in the milk, and bring to a boil over high heat, stirring frequently.

2 Sauté the veal and onion in a little butter for 5 minutes, without browning. Add to the sauce. Also add pepper, nutmeg, thyme and salt.

3 Simmer the sauce on the lowest possible heat, uncovered, for 1 hour. Never stir the sauce! Some sauce is bound to burn on the bottom of the pot; so long as it is not touched it will not affect the taste. Strain through a fine-mesh strainer and set aside. Discard what doesn't go through.

4 To make chicken soup: Measure half the sauce into a soup pot. Add the milk and the chicken meat and simmer, uncovered, until the chicken is tender – over rather than undercooked. Again, do not stir!

5 Purée the soup in a blender, first on low speed, then on high, until until absolutely smooth. Strain again through a fine-mesh strainer, discard what doesn't go through.

6 Stir in the cream and garnish with chopped parsley.

Variations:
For fish or shellfish soup: substitute 1 pound of fish or shellfish in stage 4. Cook till tender and proceed with stages 5 and 6.
For vegetable soups: substitute 1 pound of fresh vegetables (sautéed in butter) in stage 4. Cook till tender, then proceed with stages 5 and 6.
For mushroom soup: substitute 1 pound of fresh, sliced, sautéed mushrooms in stage 4. No further cooking is needed! Eliminate stage 5. Proceed with stage 6.

Note The leftover sauce keeps for several days in the refrigerator, or can be frozen for months.
The soup can be made ahead and reheated (or frozen) up to stage 5.

32

CREME DE VOLAILLE

BRUSSELS SPROUT

Chicken

Bon Appétit

This is the classic recipe for cream soup of any type. It is based on the
extremely versatile Béchamel Sauce, and since it is a little time consuming to
prepare, a double recipe for sauce has been given.
This recipe makes a sinfully rich soup – absolutely the creamiest you will
ever taste!

4 tbsp. butter
1 pound onions, cut into thin rings
1 clove garlic, crushed (optional)
2 tsp. sugar
3 tbsp. flour
7 cups beef or chicken stock, or bouillon
5 fl. oz. white wine
1 tsp. dried thyme
1 bayleaf
2 tbsp. dry sherry
8 slices French bread
1 cup grated Swiss or parmesan cheese   Serves 8

1 Melt the butter in a heavy saucepan. Add the sliced onion and chopped garlic. Sauté, covered, over a fairly low heat, for 20 minutes. Stir once in a while with a wooden spoon.

2 Uncover the pot, raise the heat a little and add the sugar. Cook for 10 minutes, stirring now and then. (The idea is *not* to let the sugar burn, just to caramelize it to give the soup a rich color.)

3 Sprinkle the flour over the onions. Stir it around well.

4 Add the stock to the pot, also the wine, thyme and bayleaf. Bring to a boil, skimming off any scum that rises to the surface. Partially cover the pot and simmer the soup for 30 minutes.

5 Just before serving, add the sherry.

The garnish;
Cut the bread into 1-inch-thick slices and toast them on a baking sheet in a 325° oven about 30 minutes, until they are completely dry. (Rub them with a cut clove of garlic after 15 minutes if desired.)
Place a piece of toast onto each bowl of soup. Sprinkle some grated cheese on top of each, and place the bowls under the broiler for a few minutes to brown the cheese slightly.

skim off scum

Butter

sliced onion
chopped garlic

Sugar

Flour

thyme

bayleaf

STOCK

White Wine

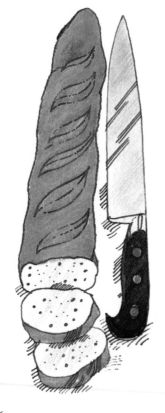

Sher[ry]

Note Onion Soup can be made ahead and frozen up to stage 4.

SOUPE À L'OIGNON GRATINÉE

The French Onion Seller

Onion Soup is generally considered French, though why exactly is uncertain. Every country has some form of onion soup, not too different one from another. This heartwarming, juicy soup has enjoyed centuries of popularity. Maybe your appreciation will more than equal Monsieur Bovary's, who in Gustave Flaubert's *Madame Bovary* returns home to find that "For dinner there was onion soup . . . and rubbed his hands together in satisfaction and said cheerfully, 'It is good to be home again!'"

2 tbsp. oil
1–2 pounds lamb for boiling (some nice bones included) in one piece
11 cups beef stock or bouillon
1 large onion, chopped
3 medium carrots, chopped
2 stalks celery, chopped
3 tbsp. butter
1 tsp. dried thyme
1 bayleaf
¼ cup pearl barley
4 oz. fresh or frozen peas
salt and pepper to taste

Serves 8–10

1 Heat the oil in a large soup pot and brown the meat in it on all sides. When nicely browned, pour on the stock or bouillon. Bring the mixture to a boil.

2 Meanwhile, sauté the onion, carrot and celery in the butter for 5–8 minutes. Add them to the soup pot.

3 Also add the thyme, bayleaf and barley. Simmer, partially covered, for 1½ hours.

THYME 1 tsp
1 BAYLEAF &
BARLEY

SKIM AS NECESSARY

Oil

lamb

Stock

RETURN LEAN MEAT

peas

MEAT
CUT OFF BONE, FAT &
GRISTLE

Season with salt & pepper

SAUTÉ in
BUTTER

1 large onion
chopped

3 medium
carrots chopped

2 stalks celery, chopped

10 minutes before the end of cooking time, add the peas. Remove the meat, and when cool enough to handle, cut off the bone, fat and gristle and discard. Return any lean meat, chopped into small pieces, to the soup.

5 Season to taste with salt and pepper.

Note Scotch Broth freezes and reheats very well.

SCOTCH BROTH

A beautiful soup, hearty, hale and healthy, a basic soup that has its origin in simple country fare. Dr. Johnson gave recognition to the dish on his tour of Scotland in 1773. Try it on a cold, frosty day, in front of the fire.

1–1½ pounds smoked pork hocks *or* **a ham bone with some meat**
10 cups cold water
1 medium carrot, finely chopped
1 medium onion, finely chopped
3 tbsp. butter or margarine
1 pound dried split green peas
salt, pepper and nutmeg to taste
chicken stock or bouillon as needed

Serves 6

SMOKED PORK HOCKS

SKIM OFF THE SCUM

3 When the meat is tender, add the vegetables to the soup pot. Also add the washed peas. Simmer the soup, uncovered, for 20–30 minutes, or until the peas are tender. Skim the soup several times if necessary.

4 Remove the meat from the pot and leave to cool a little. Then cut any lean meat off the bone and cut it into tiny shreds. Discard bone, fat and gristle.

1 Place the meat in a large pot and add the cold water. Bring to boil, cover, and simmer until the meat is tender (2 hours for pork hocks, 1 hour for ham bone).

SMOKED PORK HOCKS

5 Purée the soup in a blender, first on low speed, then turn to high until the soup is absolutely smooth.

WATER

2 Meanwhile, sauté the carrot and onion in the butter for 5 minutes.

BUTTER

6 Return the soup to soup pot. Bring back to a boil and simmer a few more minutes. Skim off the scum as it appears. Add the meat.

7 If the soup is too thick at this point, thin it down with chicken stock or bouillon to the desired consistency.

Season to taste with salt, pepper and nutmeg.

finely chopped

finely chopped

Note Excellent reheated, and freezes well.

Variations: Instead of the split green peas, use: 1 pound lentils; 1 pound kidney beans; 1 pound black beans (soak these overnight); 1 pound navy beans; 1 pound split yellow peas; or 1 pound dried lima beans.

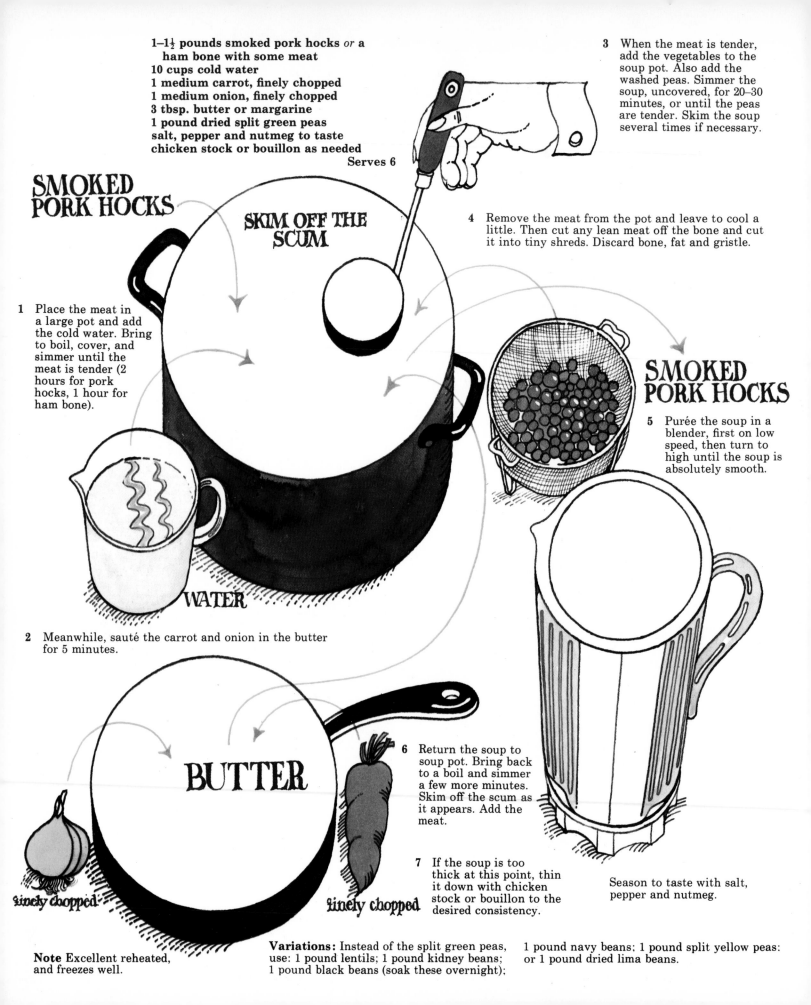

ERWTENSOEP

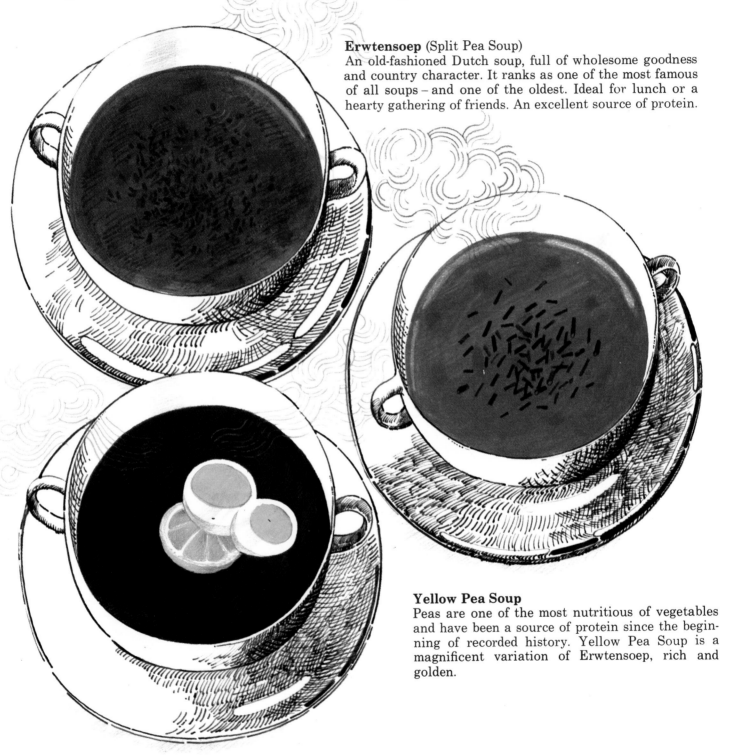

Erwtensoep (Split Pea Soup)
An old-fashioned Dutch soup, full of wholesome goodness and country character. It ranks as one of the most famous of all soups – and one of the oldest. Ideal for lunch or a hearty gathering of friends. An excellent source of protein.

Yellow Pea Soup
Peas are one of the most nutritious of vegetables and have been a source of protein since the beginning of recorded history. Yellow Pea Soup is a magnificent variation of Erwtensoep, rich and golden.

Black Bean Soup
Black beans are cultivated in the southern United States. They make an especially rich and excellent soup, typical of the South. Beans historically have played an important role in man's diet. 'Full of beans' was an apt and descriptive way of describing the state of health and natural good spirits derived from eating beans.
Garnishes for Black Bean Soup are traditionally hardboiled-egg slices and lemon.

39

2 tbsp. oil
3 large onions, roughly chopped
1–3 cloves garlic, crushed (optional)
3–4 level tablespoons paprika
2 tbsp. oil
1½ pounds lean braising (chuck) steak,
   cut into 1-inch cubes
3 medium carrots, chopped
1 pound tomatoes, peeled and roughly
   chopped or 1 can (16 oz.) tomatoes with
   their liquid
5 cups beef stock or bouillon
2 large potatoes, cubed
½ tsp. caraway seeds
½ tsp. dried marjoram
1 bayleaf
salt and pepper to taste
chopped parsley for
   garnish
        Serves 4–5

1 In a large saucepan sauté the onion in the oil until soft and transparent. Add the garlic, if used, and sauté 1 minute longer.

2 Off the heat (when the bubbling has subsided), add the paprika. Stir until all the onions are coated with it. Set aside.

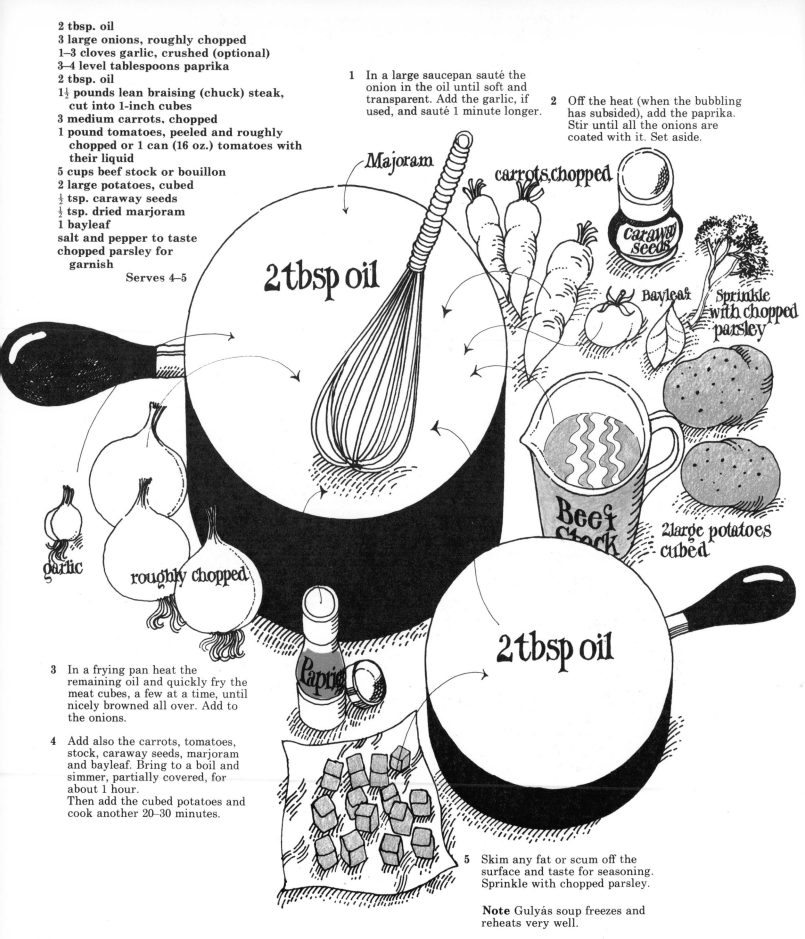

Majoram

carrots, chopped

caraway seeds

Bayleaf

Sprinkle with chopped parsley

2 tbsp oil

Beef Stock

2 large potatoes cubed

garlic

roughly chopped

Paprika

2 tbsp oil

3 In a frying pan heat the remaining oil and quickly fry the meat cubes, a few at a time, until nicely browned all over. Add to the onions.

4 Add also the carrots, tomatoes, stock, caraway seeds, marjoram and bayleaf. Bring to a boil and simmer, partially covered, for about 1 hour.
Then add the cubed potatoes and cook another 20–30 minutes.

5 Skim any fat or scum off the surface and taste for seasoning. Sprinkle with chopped parsley.

Note Gulyás soup freezes and reheats very well.

HUNGARIAN GULYÁS SOUP

Hungary is famous for its many versions of Gulyás, all hearty, down-to-earth country stews that echo the flavor of Hungarian life. Gulyás soup is born of simple peasant fare and probably evolved as the Magyar tribes roamed central Europe several centuries ago. This soup you will find as colorful and as appetizing to the palate as it is to the eye. Great with a little gypsy music.

2 half chicken breasts
10 cups chicken stock or bouillon
1 large onion, finely chopped
2 medium carrots, finely chopped
2 stalks celery (with leaves
  if possible), finely chopped
1 bayleaf

3 tbsp. butter or margarine
3 tbsp. flour
1–2 tbsp. curry powder
⅜ cup long-grain rice, cooked
salt and pepper to taste
chopped parsley for garnish

Serves 8

3 Sprinkle the vegetables with the flour and curry powder. Stir well with a wooden spoon until all the vegetables are coated. Then, with a wire whisk, stir the vegetables into the soup pot. Stir well to dissolve the flour and curry. Bring to a boil and simmer, partially covered, for 30 minutes.

1 Place the chicken breasts and the stock or bouillon in a large soup pot. Bring to a boil, and simmer *very* gently, partially covered, until chicken breasts are tender (about 20 minutes). Remove chicken breasts, and when cool enough to handle, skin and bone them. Cut the meat into tiny shreds and reserve. Leave the cooking liquid in the soup pot.

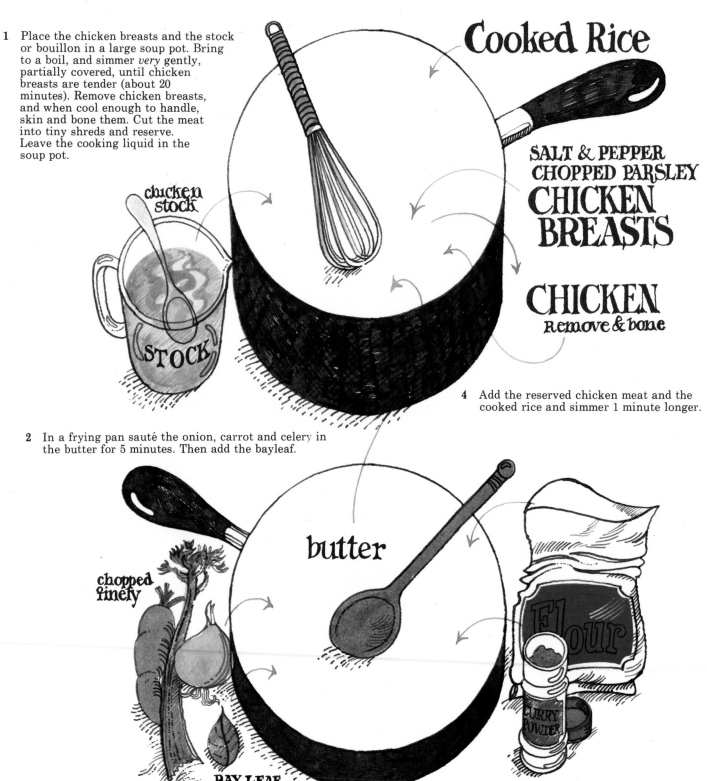

Cooked Rice

SALT & PEPPER
CHOPPED PARSLEY
CHICKEN
BREASTS

CHICKEN
Remove & bone

chicken stock

STOCK

4 Add the reserved chicken meat and the cooked rice and simmer 1 minute longer.

2 In a frying pan sauté the onion, carrot and celery in the butter for 5 minutes. Then add the bayleaf.

chopped finely

butter

Flour

CURRY POWDER

BAY LEAF

Season to taste with salt and pepper.
Garnish with chopped parsley.
Note This soup reheats very well, and even freezes.

42

Mulligatawny

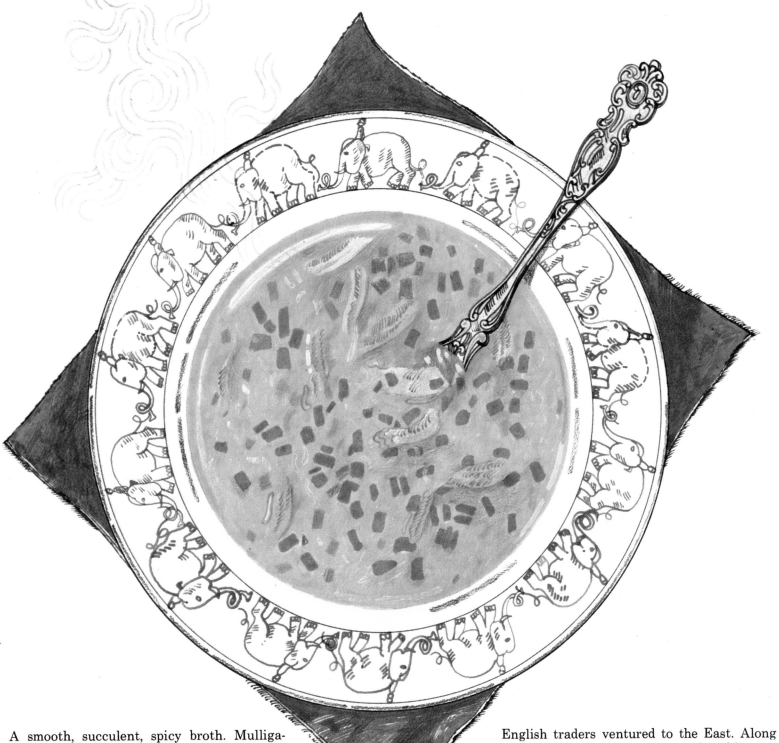

A smooth, succulent, spicy broth. Mulliga-tawny is a semi-Indian dish, one of many that originated as Dutch, Portuguese, French and English traders ventured to the East. Along with other such curry recipes, it found its way to Europe in the 18th century.

2 pounds cut-up oxtails
4 tbsp. oil
5 tbsp. flour
9 cups beef stock or bouillon
1 onion, chopped
2 carrots, chopped
1 stalk celery, chopped
1 bayleaf
1 tsp. dried thyme or marjoram
1 clove garlic, crushed (optional)
1 large potato, cubed
1 tbsp. tomato puree
salt and pepper to taste
2 tbsp. unsalted butter
2–6 tbsp. dry sherry or Madeira (optional)   Serves 8

1 Sauté the oxtails in the oil until nicely browned all over. Remove and drain on paper towels.

2 To the remaining fat add the flour and stir until the flour has acquired a nice, rich, brown color. (Stir only once in a while, because only the flour on the bottom will color; it needs "turning over" to brown the rest.) Slowly add the stock or bouillon, stirring all the time with a wire whisk. Bring to a boil, skim off the scum and fat, and add the onion, carrot, celery, bayleaf, thyme or marjoram, garlic, potato and tomato purée, and the reserved oxtails. Simmer the soup, partially covered, for 2–3 hours. Skim again if necessary.

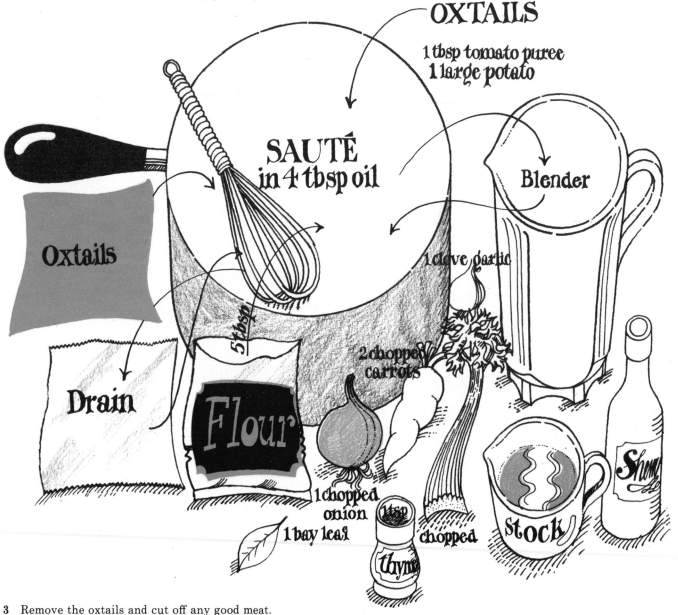

OXTAILS

3 Remove the oxtails and cut off any good meat. Discard bones, fat and gristle. Reserve meat.

4 Purée the soup in a blender, return to the soup pot and add the reserved meat to it. Reheat, skimming off any scum and fat that may rise to the surface. Season with salt and pepper.

5 Off the heat, and only just before serving, stir in the soft, unsalted butter and the sherry or Madeira.

Note Can be made ahead or frozen up to stage 4.

44

Oxtail Soup

It is a little difficult to pin-point the origins of Oxtail Soup. Certainly the ox was one of the earliest of all domesticated animals and as such became part of man's diet, the meat of the ox being used in many ways, one such being soup, as this Chinese poem, dated 3rd century B.C. suggests:

*"Ribs of the fatted ox cooked tender and succulent,
   sour and bitter blended in the soup of Wu."

This soup is delicious, and overdoing the sherry won't hurt a bit!

*(Birch & Keene, *Anthology of Chinese Literature*)

4 tbsp. butter or margarine
1 pound fresh okra, sliced or two
   10-oz. packages frozen okra, sliced
2 tbsp. butter or margarine
1 large onion, chopped
1 green pepper, chopped
1 clove garlic, crushed
2 tbsp. flour
4 cups chicken stock or bouillon
4 tomatoes, skinned, seeded and
   chopped or one 16-oz. can
   tomatoes, well drained and chopped

2 parsley sprigs } tied together
1 bayleaf
½ tsp. dried thyme
salt and pepper to taste
3 or 4 half chicken breasts
2 tbsp. Worcestershire sauce
chopped parsley for garnish
                    Serves 8

optional:
½ cup rice, cooked
   and hot
½ cup heavy
   cream

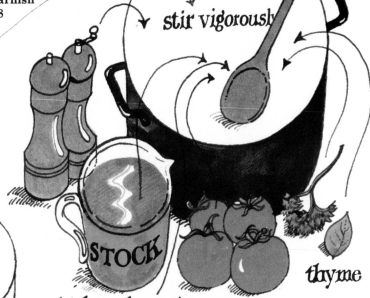

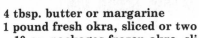

stir often

Butter

okra

3 Now pour the stock over the vegetables and stir vigorously. Add the sautéed okra slices, tomatoes, parsley and bayleaf, thyme, salt and pepper. Also add the skinned chicken breasts. Bring to a boil and then simmer, partially covered, for about 30 minutes, or until the meat is tender.

4 Remove the chicken and cut the meat into small cubes. Return to pot. Add the Worcestershire sauce and taste for seasoning. Do not boil again!

1 In a frying pan melt the butter or margarine. In it sauté the okra slices. Sauté them until the stringiness, that will show itself as white threads due to the heat, disappears. Stir often (cook about 15 minutes). Set aside.

stir often

Flour

Butter

garlic

onion~ chopped

TASTE FOR SEASONING

5 Add the cream, if used. If desired, place a tablespoon of hot rice into each soup plate and ladle the soup over it. Sprinkle with parsley.

Note This soup reheats and freezes well.

2 In a soup pot melt the remaining butter. In it sauté the onion and green pepper for 5 minutes, stirring often. Add the garlic and sauté 1 minute longer. Sprinkle the flour over the vegetables. Stir until all of it has been absorbed.

SOUTHERN CHICKEN GUMBO

chop
onion
4 tomatoes
1 pepper
bouillon
Chicken Stock
1 clove garlic
Okra
3 half chicken breasts
bay leaf
Chicken Breast
thyme
2 sprigs parsley

Gumbos (poultry, meat, fish or shellfish) are typical of Creole cooking with okra added to give the soup its glutinous quality. The soup evolved from a Choctaw Indian dish.

Bon Appetit

1½ pounds soup beef with bone *or*
one 2–3 pound chicken
5 cups cold water
1 tsp. salt
½ tsp. pepper
1 large stalk celery, roughly chopped
1 large carrot, roughly chopped
1 large onion, roughly chopped
2 parsley sprigs
1 bayleaf
½ tsp. dried marjoram
4 tbsp. alphabet noodles, cooked
finely chopped parsley for garnish

Serves 4

1 Place the soup beef (or chicken) in a large saucepan. Add the cold water, salt, pepper, celery, carrot, onion, parsley sprig, bayleaf and marjoram. Bring to a boil and skim if necessary. Simmer the soup, partially covered, 2 hours for beef, 1 hour for chicken. Remove meat or chicken.

2 Strain the soup through a fine-mesh strainer. Discard all the vegetables. Return broth to pot.

3 Cut any lean meat off the soup beef, discarding any bone or fat. If a chicken is used, remove 1 chicken breast, skin and bone it and cut into tiny shreds. Reserve.

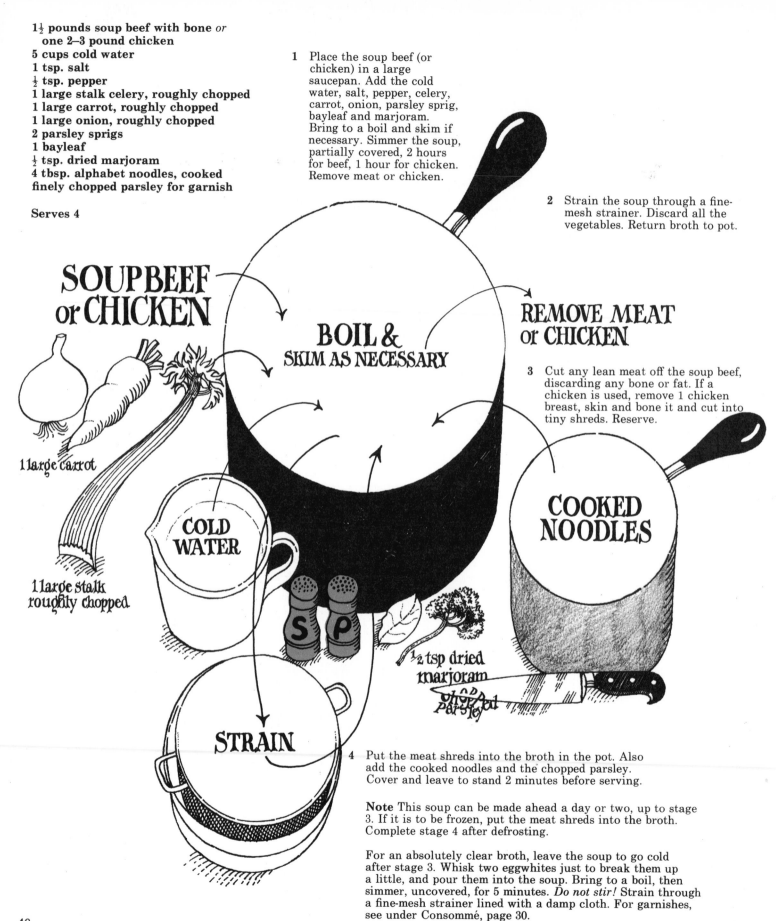

SOUP BEEF or CHICKEN

1 large carrot

1 large stalk roughly chopped

COLD WATER

BOIL & SKIM AS NECESSARY

REMOVE MEAT or CHICKEN

COOKED NOODLES

½ tsp dried marjoram
chopped parsley

STRAIN

4 Put the meat shreds into the broth in the pot. Also add the cooked noodles and the chopped parsley. Cover and leave to stand 2 minutes before serving.

Note This soup can be made ahead a day or two, up to stage 3. If it is to be frozen, put the meat shreds into the broth. Complete stage 4 after defrosting.

For an absolutely clear broth, leave the soup to go cold after stage 3. Whisk two eggwhites just to break them up a little, and pour them into the soup. Bring to a boil, then simmer, uncovered, for 5 minutes. *Do not stir!* Strain through a fine-mesh strainer lined with a damp cloth. For garnishes, see under Consommé, page 30.

FLEISCHBRÜHE

This is an old German soup that has been a hot favorite with countless generations of children. Since its ingredients consist of simple country fare, this recipe or a variation would almost certainly have been popular when Dr. Hoffmann wrote his classic children's story, *Struwwelpeter* in 1844, from which "The Story of Augustus who would not have any soup" is taken. It is a poem that testifies to the importance soup played in a child's diet. Though it is difficult to imagine that this particular soup would have been rejected by Augustus. Ever! This old recipe remains very easy to prepare, is full of nutrition and is a firm favorite with our own children and their friends.

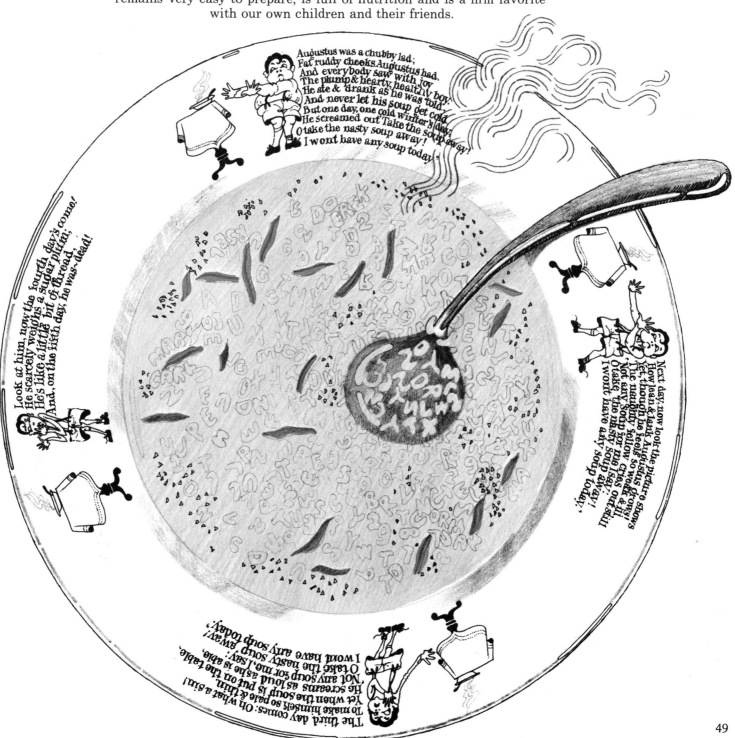

Augustus was a chubby lad;
Fat ruddy cheeks Augustus had.
And everybody saw with joy
The plump & hearty healthy boy.
He ate & drank as he was told;
And never let his soup get cold.
But one day, one cold winter's day,
He screamed out 'Take the soup away!
O take the nasty soup away!
I won't have any soup today.'

Next day, now look the picture shows
How lean & lank Augustus grows!
Yet, though he feels so weak & ill,
The naughty fellow cries out still
'Not any soup for me, I say!
O take the nasty soup away!
I won't have any soup today.'

The third day comes: Oh what a sin!
To make himself so pale & thin,
Yet when the soup is put on the table,
He screams as loud as he is able,
'Not any soup for me, I say!
O take the nasty soup away!
I won't have any soup today.'

Look at him, now the fourth day's come!
He scarcely weighs a sugar plum;
He's like a little bit of thread,
And, on the fifth day, he was—dead!

**1 package chicken-noodle-soup mix
2 ripe avocados
½ small onion, very finely chopped
1 cup light cream (or half and half)
lemon wedges for garnish
chopped chives for garnish (optional)
juice of ½ lemon (for dipping)
a little salt and pepper if necessary**

Serves 4–5

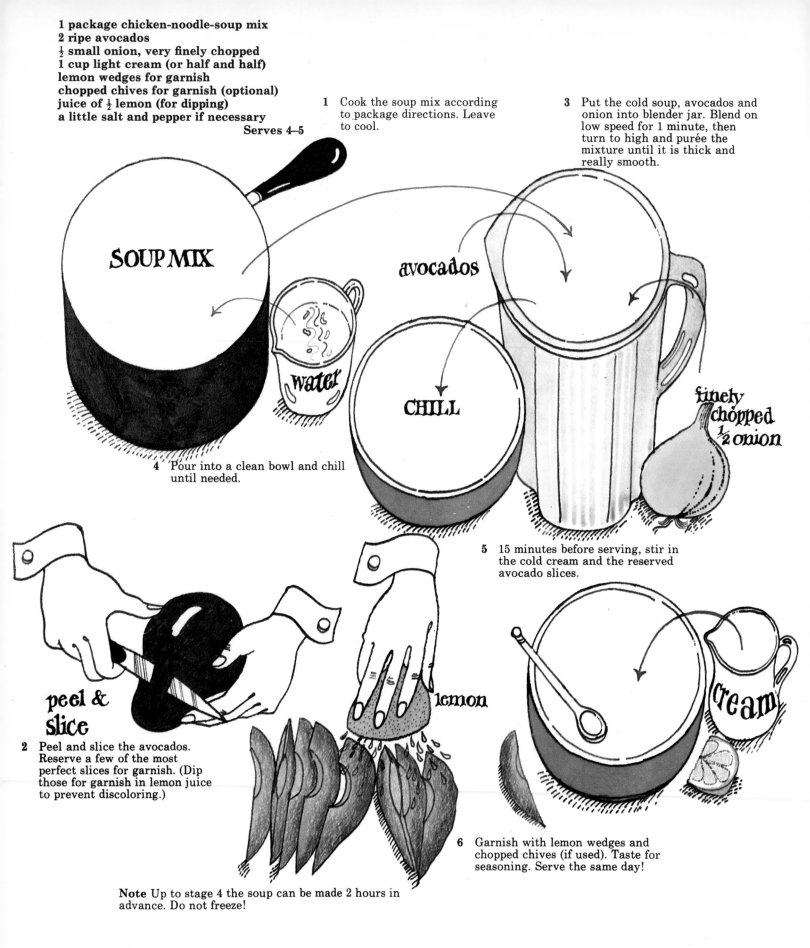

1 Cook the soup mix according to package directions. Leave to cool.

3 Put the cold soup, avocados and onion into blender jar. Blend on low speed for 1 minute, then turn to high and purée the mixture until it is thick and really smooth.

SOUP MIX

water

avocados

CHILL

finely chopped ½ onion

4 Pour into a clean bowl and chill until needed.

5 15 minutes before serving, stir in the cold cream and the reserved avocado slices.

peel & slice

lemon

cream

2 Peel and slice the avocados. Reserve a few of the most perfect slices for garnish. (Dip those for garnish in lemon juice to prevent discoloring.)

6 Garnish with lemon wedges and chopped chives (if used). Taste for seasoning. Serve the same day!

Note Up to stage 4 the soup can be made 2 hours in advance. Do not freeze!

CALIFORNIAN AVOCADO SOUP

A very delicate soup, cool and refined. Ideal for a hot summer's day, this soup makes a superb start to a meal. Surprise and delight your friends with this extraordinary, subtle taste. Escoffier once said "Of all the items on the menu, soup is that which exacts the most delicate perfection and the strictest attention." This soup will stand the closest scrutiny and leave a lasting impression.

1 piece beef for boiling (1½–2 pounds), lean
7 cups beef stock or bouillon
1 marrow bone (optional)
one 1-pound can tomatoes and their juice, chopped
1 stalk celery with leaves, cut into julienne strips
2 sprigs parsley ⎫
2 bay leaves ⎬ tied together
10 peppercorns ⎭
1 pound green cabbage, shredded
2 medium carrots, cut into julienne strips

2 medium onions, chopped
1 tsp. dried dill
¼ (or less) tsp. caraway seeds
½ cup red wine (optional)
2 tbsp. vinegar
1 tsp. sugar
1 pound cooked beets, fresh or canned (including juice), cut into julienne strips
½ cup sour cream

Serves 5–6

1 Place the meat (and bone, if used) into a large pot. Cover with stock and bring to a boil over high heat. Skim off any scum that rises to the surface. Simmer the meat, partially covered, for about 1 hour. Remove the bone and discard.

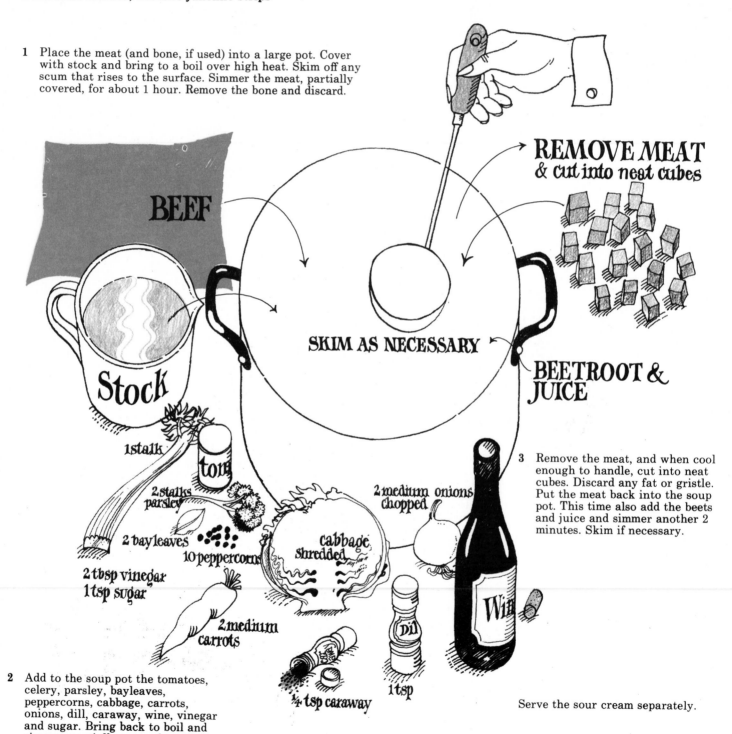

BEEF

Stock

REMOVE MEAT
& cut into neat cubes

SKIM AS NECESSARY

BEETROOT &
JUICE

1 stalk
tom
2 stalks parsley
2 bay leaves
10 peppercorns
2 tbsp vinegar
1 tsp sugar
2 medium carrots
cabbage shredded
2 medium onions chopped
Dil
Win
¼ tsp caraway
1 tsp

3 Remove the meat, and when cool enough to handle, cut into neat cubes. Discard any fat or gristle. Put the meat back into the soup pot. This time also add the beets and juice and simmer another 2 minutes. Skim if necessary.

2 Add to the soup pot the tomatoes, celery, parsley, bayleaves, peppercorns, cabbage, carrots, onions, dill, caraway, wine, vinegar and sugar. Bring back to boil and simmer, partially covered, until the vegetables are tender (30–40 minutes).

Serve the sour cream separately.

Note Borscht improves when reheated. It can also be frozen.

52

PEPPERCORNS

Dill

SOUR CREAM

Caraway

RUSSIAN BORSCHT

Borscht is Russia's most famous main-dish soup, full of robust goodness, with an unusual flavor. The addition of beets gives it a gloriously red color which contrasts beautifully with the traditional garnish of sour cream.

for the dough
2 cups plain flour
2 large eggs
1 tsp. oil
a little cold water, if needed
for the filling
10 oz. fresh or frozen spinach
leaves
1 pound minced pork

1 tsp. dried ground ginger
2 spring onions, finely chopped
1 tsp. oil
3 tsp. soy sauce
salt and pepper to taste
a little dry sherry (optional)
for the soup
6–7 cups hot, well-flavored chicken
stock, (*not* bouillon)
a little chopped parsley for garnish
Serves 6–8

1 Cook the spinach leaves in salted water till tender. Drain. Pick out a few nice leaves for garnish and reserve. Put the rest back in the pot, and over a medium heat dry them until all the water has evaporated. Chop finely.

2 Make a dough by combining the flour, eggs, oil and, if needed, a little cold water. Knead it on a flat surface for a few moments. Shape into a ball and wrap in plastic. Refrigerate for ½ hour.

3 Mix together the spinach, pork, ginger, spring onions, oil, soy sauce, salt, pepper and sherry (if used). Mix till well blended.

4 Roll out the dough on a lightly floured surface as thin as you can. Cut into 2-inch circles (or squares or triangles).

5 Place 1 teaspoon of the filling onto each piece of dough and brush the edges with cold water. Now press the edges together to enclose the filling all around. Seal the seams well.

6 Drop the wontons into a pot of boiling, salted water. Simmer them, partially covered, for about 15 minutes.

7 Meanwhile, heat the chicken stock and transfer the cooked wontons to it with a slotted spoon. Also add the reserved spinach leaves.

8 Sprinkle with chopped parsley and serve piping hot.

Note Best when fresh. Soup can be reheated if necessary, but do not freeze.

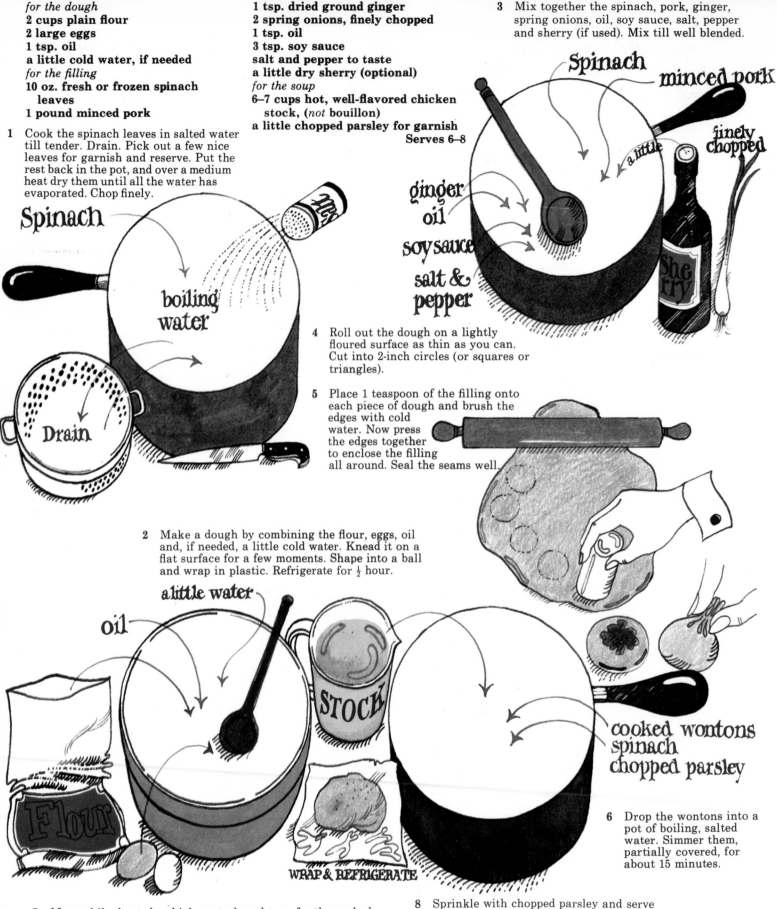

54

CHINESE WONTON SOUP

Wonton Soup is a popular main-dish soup from China, a steaming hot broth, with melt-in-the-mouth dumplings filled with a spicy meat mixture. Truly delightful for an informal dinner party.

2–3 pounds chuck steak *or* **pot roast, tied securely with string**
1 pound chicken backs and necks
11 cups cold water
2 large carrots, chopped
1 medium turnip, chopped
2 leeks, sliced
1 stalk celery, chopped
1 large onion, chopped
2 parsley sprigs ⎫
1 large bayleaf ⎭ **tied together**
½ tsp. dried thyme
salt and pepper to taste
1 cut-up marrow bone, tied in a muslin or cheesecloth bag

Serves 4

1 Place the beef and chicken backs and necks in a heavy pot. Pour over the cold water. Bring to a boil over medium heat. As the scum appears, skim it off, and keep skimming for several minutes, until the surface is clear. Now add the vegetables and the bundle of parsley and bayleaf, the thyme and some salt and pepper.

2 Partially cover the pot and simmer the soup over the lowest possible heat. Do not let it bubble at all at the sides, cook it really gently! Simmer for 3 hours.

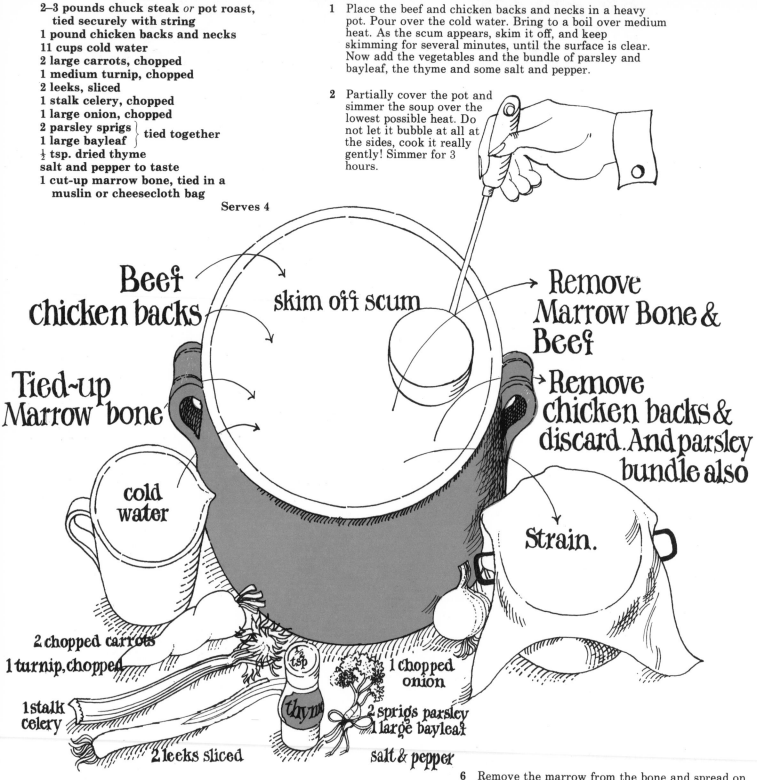

Beef
chicken backs

skim off scum

Remove
Marrow Bone &
Beef

Tied-up
Marrow bone

Remove
chicken backs &
discard. And parsley
bundle also

cold
water

Strain.

2 chopped carrots
1 turnip, chopped

1 stalk
celery

1 chopped
onion

tsp
thyme

2 sprigs parsley
1 large bayleaf

2 leeks sliced

salt & pepper

3 Add the tied-up marrow-bone, and simmer another ½ hour.

4 Remove marrow bone and beef and reserve. Remove chicken backs and necks and parsley bundle and discard.

5 Strain the broth through a fine-mesh strainer lined with a damp cloth and discard all the vegetables. Taste the broth for seasoning and degrease as much as you can.

6 Remove the marrow from the bone and spread on hot toast before serving.

Note The broth is served ladled over croutons (see Bouillabaisse, page 14) in shallow soup plates. (Or use any of the garnishes for clear soups; see Consommé, page 30.)
The beef is served carved as a second course and traditionally served with boiled potatoes and cabbage. And some garnish, like sour gherkins, coarse salt, mustard, horseradish or tomato sauce. Reheats well!
Leftover broth freezes well!

56

POT·AU·FEU

An extremely old French peasant soup of which there are several regional variations. This classic Pot-au-Feu is made of beef and chicken. In some regions of France it is customary to add veal, pork and sometimes mutton.

Like the stockpot, Pot-au-Feu evolved from the cauldron, into which all manner of ingredients were tossed every day. The pot was hung over a fire that was never put out, thus providing an ever-changing broth.

1½ pounds firm, fresh, red cherries
4 whole cloves
1 cinnamon stick or ½ tsp. ground
  cinnamon
juice of 1 lemon
1 piece of lemon rind
4 tbsp. sugar
2 cups cold water
3 tbsp. cornflour
1 glass port or burgundy   **Serves 4**

4 Crack the cherry stones with a sharp blow of a hammer and place them in a small saucepan. Add the port or burgundy, bring to a boil – then remove from heat, cover, and leave to infuse for 15–20 minutes. Strain through a fine-mesh strainer and reserve the liquid. Discard stones.

1 Put the cherries, cloves, cinnamon, lemon juice and lemon rind, sugar and water into a soup pot. Bring to a boil and simmer, partially covered, until the cherries are tender (15–25 minutes).

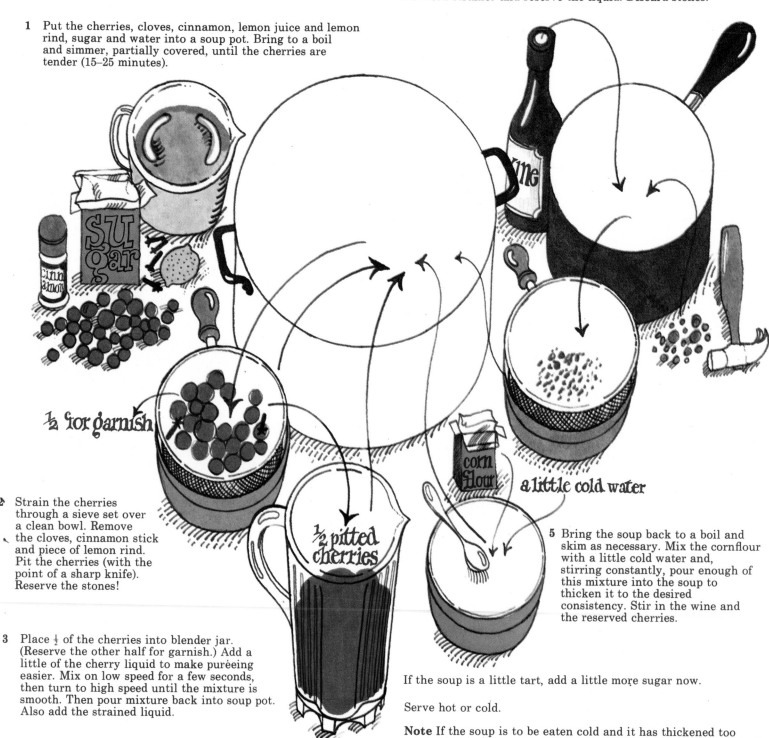

½ for garnish

½ pitted cherries

corn flour

a little cold water

2 Strain the cherries through a sieve set over a clean bowl. Remove the cloves, cinnamon stick and piece of lemon rind. Pit the cherries (with the point of a sharp knife). Reserve the stones!

5 Bring the soup back to a boil and skim as necessary. Mix the cornflour with a little cold water and, stirring constantly, pour enough of this mixture into the soup to thicken it to the desired consistency. Stir in the wine and the reserved cherries.

3 Place ½ of the cherries into blender jar. (Reserve the other half for garnish.) Add a little of the cherry liquid to make puréeing easier. Mix on low speed for a few seconds, then turn to high speed until the mixture is smooth. Then pour mixture back into soup pot. Also add the strained liquid.

If the soup is a little tart, add a little more sugar now.

Serve hot or cold.

Note If the soup is to be eaten cold and it has thickened too much, thin it down with a little port or burgundy. Eat same day! Blueberries can be substituted for the cherries.

KIRSCHSUPPE

A magnificent German soup. Absolutely delicious – try this soup when cherries are in season. It's a special summer flavor typical of German cooking – with a taste you can't afford to miss!

5 tbsp sugar
1 small piece lemon peel
½ tsp. powdered cinnamon
2 cloves
1½ cups milk
one 12-oz. can dark or lager beer
4 tbsp. cornflour
½ cup heavy cream
1 egg yolk
1 tbsp. brandy (optional)
1 egg white (optional)

Serves 4

1 Place sugar, lemon peel, cinnamon and cloves in heavy saucepan. Pour over the milk and beer. Leave uncovered and bring to a boil, stirring a little so as not to burn the sugar.

2 Mix the cornflour with enough water to make a smooth pouring consistency, and pour enough of this into the soup (stirring all the time with a wire whisk) to reach the desired thickness. The soup should be just thickened enough to coat the back of a spoon. Boil for just half a minute. Remove from heat.

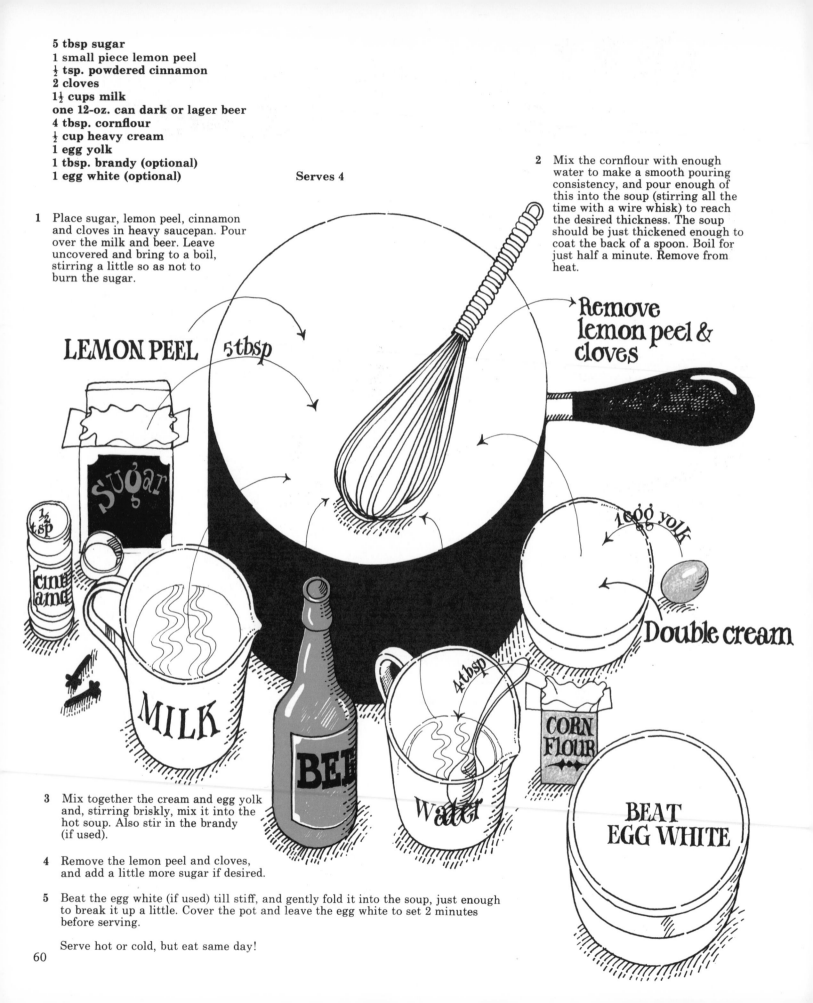

LEMON PEEL

5 tbsp

Remove lemon peel & cloves

sugar

1 egg yolk

Double cream

MILK

BEER

4 tbsp

Water

CORN FLOUR

BEAT EGG WHITE

3 Mix together the cream and egg yolk and, stirring briskly, mix it into the hot soup. Also stir in the brandy (if used).

4 Remove the lemon peel and cloves, and add a little more sugar if desired.

5 Beat the egg white (if used) till stiff, and gently fold it into the soup, just enough to break it up a little. Cover the pot and leave the egg white to set 2 minutes before serving.

Serve hot or cold, but eat same day!

Biersuppe

Guten Appetit

Biersuppe is a typically German soup, that in all probability dates back several centuries. It is further testimony to the German love of beer. In Germany, it is usually made with dark beer, which has a very low alcohol content. Mostly it is eaten hot, usually preceding a cold evening meal. When made with lager beer, it is best eaten well chilled.

STOCKS

Beef Stock

5–6 pounds beef bones (shin and marrow mixture)
2 pigs feet, split in half
4 quarts cold water
½ pound carrots, chopped
½ pound onions, chopped
2 stalks celery, chopped
2 parsley sprigs ⎫ tied together
1 bayleaf ⎭
1 tsp. dried thyme

Place the bones and pigs feet into a large pot. Cover them with the cold water.
   Bring the pot to a boil over high heat. As the scum appears on the surface, skim it off see under Skimming. Keep skimming it for about 30 minutes, until the scum ceases to rise. (You don't have to be too careful at this point, most of the liquid being scooped up is water.) Now add the chopped vegetables and the bouquet garnie and simmer the stock, only partially covered, for 8 hours.
   Strain the stock through a damp cloth set in a sieve over a large pot or pail. Discard the bones and vegetables.
   Store the stock in individual 1-pint containers. It can be refrigerated for about 2 weeks, or frozen for months.

Chicken Stock

4–5 pounds chicken backs and necks
4 quarts cold water
½ pound carrots, chopped
½ pound onions, chopped
2 stalks celery, chopped
2 parsley sprigs ⎫ tied together
1 bayleaf ⎭
½ tsp. dried thyme

Place the chicken backs and necks into a large pot. Cover them with the cold water.
   Bring to a boil. As the scum appears on the surface, skim it off. Keep skimming until the scum no longer appears. (See under beef stock.)
   Add the cut-up vegetables and the bouquet garni and simmer, partially covered, for 5 hours.
   Strain and store as for beef stock.

Fish Stock

1 medium carrot, chopped
1 medium onion, chopped
1 stalk celery, chopped
1 bayleaf ⎫ tied together
2 parsley sprigs ⎭
½ tsp. dried thyme
2 pints cold water
2 pints dry white wine
3 pounds heads and tails of white fish

Place all ingredients in a large pot. Bring to a boil. As the scum appears, skim it off very carefully. (You don't want to waste any of the wine!) Skim until the scum no longer appears, otherwise the stock will be cloudy.
   Simmer the stock, partially covered, about 1 hour.
   Strain and store as for beef stock.

SALAD CONTENTS

INTRODUCTION

The Salad! A bowl of luscious, fresh greens coated with a smooth, subtle dressing. Or raw vegetables, marinated and flavored with a hint of spice or herbs. Such are the delights that can accompany the gourmet meal and family fare alike.

The salad in one form or another is a creation of infinite variety, always crisp and fresh, winter and summer alike. The sensitive palate demands a salad to accompany most meals to complement and enhance their flavor – not always a basic green salad, but one frequently making use of seasonal vegetables to give further color and imagination to a meal.

These pages are a collection of salad recipes and ideas that I hope will stimulate the reader into discovering the delights of the salad – a delight to the eye as well as to the palate. Also, for those people who are already salad devotees, I hope the variety will give them renewed interest, especially with the inclusion of many European salads with which they may not be familiar.

A good salad doesn't just happen. A lot of love and attention has to go into its preparation. Handle it gently at all times! You will be rewarded by maximum crispness. The actual tossing of the finally assembled ingredients is for many people quite a ritual, something usually done at the dinner table, with infinite care being taken not to bruise a single leaf.

The art of the salad is truly underrated. The pure tenderness of fresh greens stimulates and refreshes the palate so that what might accompany or follow a salad can be more fully appreciated. There is a kind of sincerity about a fresh salad that escapes definition – the most natural of foods eaten when, ideally, they are at their best and most nutritious – like the very humble yet versatile Green Salad, a classic recipe, or Chef's Salad, an American classic. All the salads in this book are classics of one kind or another, all from different parts of the world, all with their own individual tastes and characteristics.

I have tried to give emphasis to the use and suitability of certain vegetables at certain times of the year. When fresh, seasonal vegetables are logically at their best and cheapest. This is an added bonus, but by no means a prerequisite to the preparation of a fine salad.

Finally, whatever your motivation for discovering the salad, or re-discovering it, I trust that it will add color, imagination and enjoyment to your cooking and eating. For that is what the delights of the salad are about.

Bon appétit!

HINTS ON HOW TO MAKE YOUR SALAD A HIT

THE DO'S & DON'TS

In order that you may get the most out of your salad, the following hints will help to give guidance on the selection of ingredients and their preparation.

Lettuce
Handle it gently at all times! I have been horrified only too often to see a greengrocer stuff a tender head of lettuce into too small a paper bag, causing it to bruise. Bruises are waste – especially with Boston and romaine lettuce. These are especially fragile, Iceberg and chicory are less so.

Always wash the lettuce well, but make sure it is completely dry before tossing it with vinaigrette dressing because the dressing will not adhere to wet leaves. The best way to do this is to wrap the washed leaves in a towel (or paper towel) and leave them in the refrigerator for 2–3 hours. The towel helps to soak up the water, and the salad will

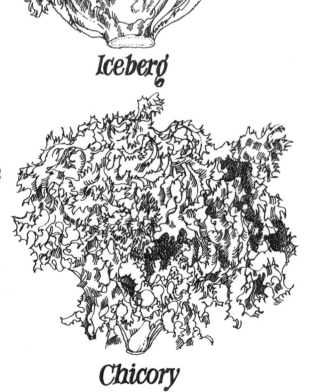

Iceberg

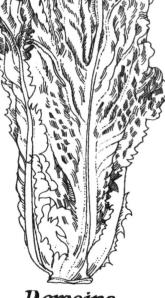

Boston Lettuce

Romaine

Chicory

The four most popular lettuces in America

come out crisp and dry. The dark in the refrigerator is also an advantage because light tends to make lettuce leaves wilt.

Another way to dry lettuce is to shake the washed leaves in a wire basket or a colander. But be gentle – don't bruise them.

Never cut lettuce with a knife, always tear it into bite-size pieces. This gives the leaves a greater absorbency along the tear.

It is best not to toss the salad until just before serving – preferably at the dinner table – since it will go limp quite quickly once it comes into contact with the oil (I cheat sometimes, when I have a lot of last-minute cooking to do. I make up the dressing in a bowl, pile the dried lettuce leaves loosely on top, and leave it in the refrigerator, covered with a paper towel, for an hour or even longer. Then all it needs is tossing, immediately before serving.)

Cucumber

Cucumbers are often bitter at the blossom end. Therefore make it a habit to cut the cucumber in half first, and peel it from the cut end to within $\frac{1}{2}$ inch of the ends. Thus you avoid pulling the bitterness all through the cucumber. Also, cucumbers shed a lot of water when they come into contact with salt, therefore it is advisable to sprinkle the peeled, sliced cucumber with some salt, leaving it to drain for at least $\frac{1}{2}$ hour in a colander. Then rinse off the salt, making sure the slices are quite dry before mixing them with the dressing.

Garlic

Some people find the use of garlic objectionable, therefore it is listed in most recipes as being optional. Only when it is not listed as optional would I suggest you really must use it, for this is the only way to catch the authentic flavor of some of these classic salads. Could it be that the smell of garlic follows you around? On your chopping board, your chopping knife, your fingers? Try sprinkling some salt on your chopping board, then dip your knife into it. Then cut or crush your garlic clove in the salt. You won't smell a thing! Sometimes it is enough to just rub a salad bowl with a cut clove of garlic; this way you don't actually eat it. Another way to give a salad a slight garlic flavor is the French way of rubbing a piece of stale bread with a cut clove of garlic and then tossing it around with the greens and the dressing. (Remove the bread before serving the salad.) This piece of bread is known as a *chapon*.

Oil

Most cookbooks will have you believe that only olive oil will do. Authentic vinaigrette dressing does indeed call for olive oil, but actually any oil found on your supermarket shelf can be used. You might even prefer it to the very heavy olive oil. Only in recipes where I specifically recommend the use of olive oil would I strongly suggest you use it for maximum authenticity.

Vinegar

The same applies to vinegar. Red or white wine vinegars are undoubtedly the most delicious. Try buying the unflavored ones though. That way you can add your own flavorings, either herbs from your garden or dried ones off your kitchen shelf. This lets you bring more variety into your dressings. Ordinary vinegars are also quite delicious, and certainly much cheaper, and added herbs give them flavor. You will find that I have used mostly ordinary vinegars in my recipes.

Instead of vinegar you can also use an equal quantity of fresh lemon juice. This can make a very pleasant change. If the lemon dressing seems a little sour, add a sprinkle of sugar to it.

Salad Bowls

The ideal salad bowl for tossed salads is a large wooden one, with a large wooden spoon and fork. The softness of the wooden utensils is least likely to bruise the salad. These bowls should be washed quickly in warm soapy water and dried straight away. Never leave one to soak.

Glass bowls are also very attractive, as are china or ceramic ones. Just make sure they are not made of a porous material; in other words, they must be well glazed. Naturally you would not let vinegar touch silver or metal bowls.

Salad Dressings

For tossed green or mixed salads only a vinaigrette dressing (oil, vinegar or lemon) is acceptable. I tend to have a personal dislike for all the creamy concoctions in bottles and jars. I find home-made ones acceptable, though only on Iceberg lettuce, since this is the only kind of lettuce that won't collapse under a heavy dressing. A salad is designed to stimulate the palate, therefore a salad with a creamy dressing tends to have the reverse effect. However, for those who can't live without creamy dressings, I have given recipes of some of the more popular ones.

As regards mayonnaise, I would like to stress that only a *good* commercial one should be used. Or better still, make your own.

Never, never use any kind of commercial salad dressing for any of the recipes in this book.

When and How to Serve

Salads can start a meal and be served as an hors d'oeuvre, go with a meal and accompany the main dish, or come after the main course. When eaten before a meal as an hors d'oeuvre, the salad should be served on individual chilled plates and eaten with just a fork. The same applies to salads eaten after the main course. Salads eaten with the main course may also be served on small individual plates or bowls and placed at the top left-hand side of the dinner plate. It is also quite acceptable to serve a salad on the same plate as the main course, especially with rice or pasta dishes, when no other vegetable is served.

One note of advice: always serve a salad at some point during a dinner party. Your guests will appreciate the fresh, cool change during the meal.

And, diet-conscious or not, a salad can make an ideal meal in itself.

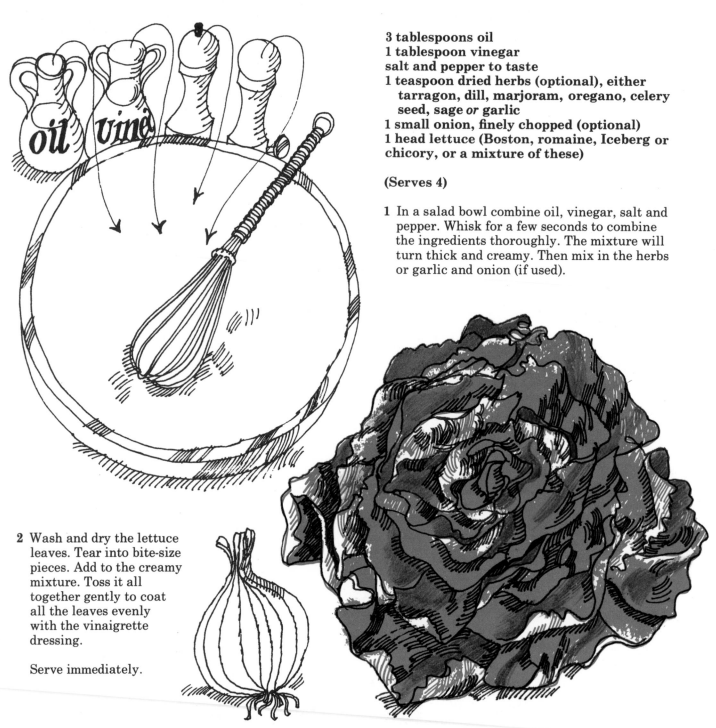

3 tablespoons oil
1 tablespoon vinegar
salt and pepper to taste
1 teaspoon dried herbs (optional), either
  tarragon, dill, marjoram, oregano, celery
  seed, sage *or* garlic
1 small onion, finely chopped (optional)
1 head lettuce (Boston, romaine, Iceberg or
chicory, or a mixture of these)

(Serves 4)

1 In a salad bowl combine oil, vinegar, salt and
pepper. Whisk for a few seconds to combine
the ingredients thoroughly. The mixture will
turn thick and creamy. Then mix in the herbs
or garlic and onion (if used).

2 Wash and dry the lettuce
leaves. Tear into bite-size
pieces. Add to the creamy
mixture. Toss it all
together gently to coat
all the leaves evenly
with the vinaigrette
dressing.

Serve immediately.

Note:
The Green Salad is also the basis for making a
Mixed Salad – simply add your own choice of
vegetables (tomato, cucumber, radishes,
watercress, mustard greens, red and green peppers,
sliced mushrooms, etc.)

The Basic Green Salad

This is probably the world's most popular and versatile salad. The classic French vinaigrette dressing gives it a tangy kind of flavor, guaranteed to refresh the palate. As a side dish the green salad will accompany any main course. It is a must with all rice and pasta dishes.

When you are not sure of a vegetable to go with a certain dish, the green salad will always prove an excellent choice.

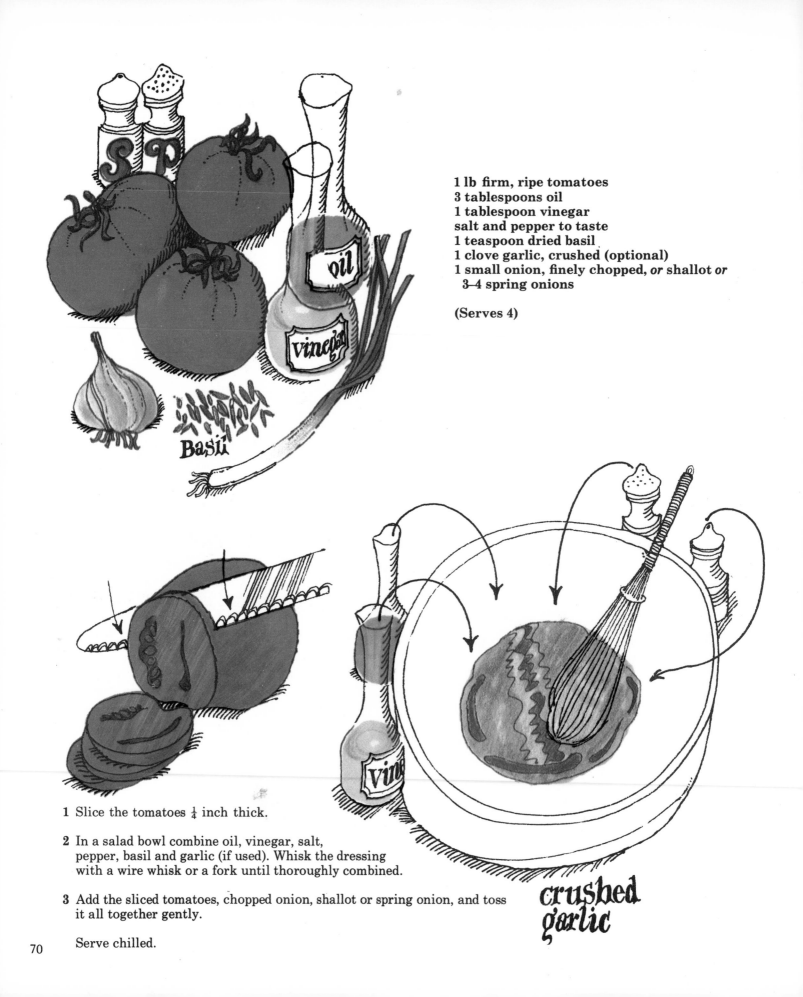

1 lb firm, ripe tomatoes
3 tablespoons oil
1 tablespoon vinegar
salt and pepper to taste
1 teaspoon dried basil
1 clove garlic, crushed (optional)
1 small onion, finely chopped, *or* shallot *or*
  3–4 spring onions

(Serves 4)

Basil

oil

vinegar

1 Slice the tomatoes ¼ inch thick.

2 In a salad bowl combine oil, vinegar, salt,
pepper, basil and garlic (if used). Whisk the dressing
with a wire whisk or a fork until thoroughly combined.

3 Add the sliced tomatoes, chopped onion, shallot or spring onion, and toss
it all together gently.

crushed
garlic

Serve chilled.

TOMATO SALAD

Especially fine in summer when tomatoes are at their peak. Cool and juicy, it is ideal for serving with fried dishes – particularly steak, chops or fish. A bowl of tomato salad will add a brilliant splash of color to the dinner table.

A touch of basil, together with the garlic, highlights the authentic Continental flavor of this recipe.

1 cucumber
2 tablespoons oil
2 tablespoons vinegar
salt and pepper to taste
$\frac{1}{4}$ teaspoon dried dill
3–4 spring onions, chopped, *or* 1 small onion, chopped
1 tablespoon heavy cream *or* evaporated milk

(Serves 4)

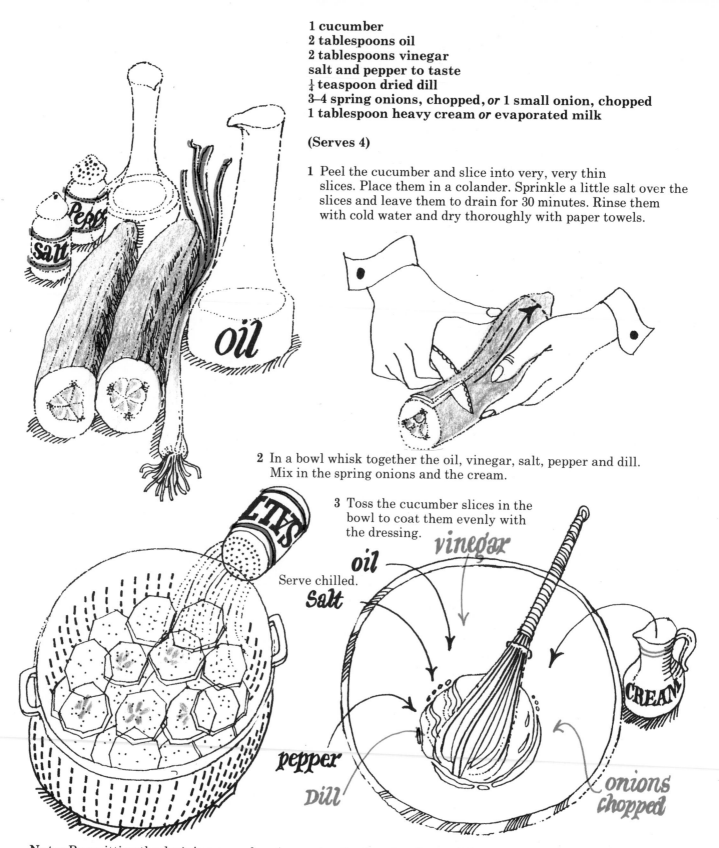

1 Peel the cucumber and slice into very, very thin
  slices. Place them in a colander. Sprinkle a little salt over the
  slices and leave them to drain for 30 minutes. Rinse them
  with cold water and dry thoroughly with paper towels.

2 In a bowl whisk together the oil, vinegar, salt, pepper and dill.
  Mix in the spring onions and the cream.

3 Toss the cucumber slices in the
  bowl to coat them evenly with
  the dressing.

Serve chilled.

Note: By omitting the draining procedure (preparing the dressing first and then slicing the peeled cucumber into it), the dressing will be diluted by the juice from the cucumber. This also makes a delicious salad, and children love the juice.

CUCUMBER SALAD

This beautifully juicy salad with a taste of
spring is very smooth on the palate and is ideal
with rice dishes or with buttered, new potatoes.
The addition of dill gives it a slightly sweet
and very delicate taste. A favorite with
children.

1 lb good, small red potatoes
2 tablespoons vinegar
½ teaspoon sugar
salt and pepper to taste

(Serves 3 or 4)

1 small onion, finely chopped
1 heaped tablespoon chopped gherkin
  (optional)
3–4 heaped tablespoons good mayonnaise
1 hardboiled egg, cut into wedges
a little chopped parsley

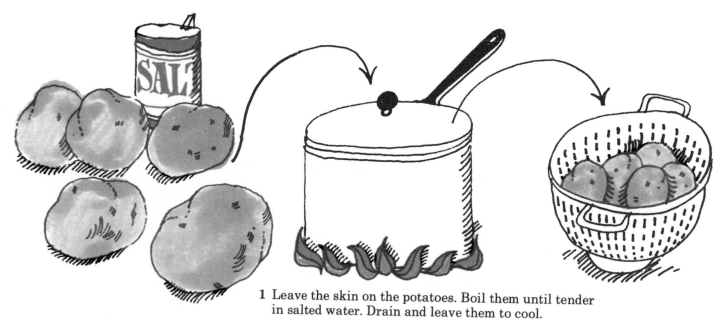

1 Leave the skin on the potatoes. Boil them until tender in salted water. Drain and leave them to cool.

2 Put the vinegar, sugar, salt and pepper into a bowl and whisk to combine. Add chopped onion and gherkin (if used) and the peeled, thinly sliced potatoes. (Halve the larger potatoes to keep all the slices small.)

3 Add the mayonnaise, mix it all well, and garnish with the hardboiled egg and chopped parsley.

4 Leave to marinate for 1 hour.

Note: This salad will keep for a day or two if kept tightly covered in a refrigerator. To freshen it up again, toss in 1 tablespoon of boiling water before serving.

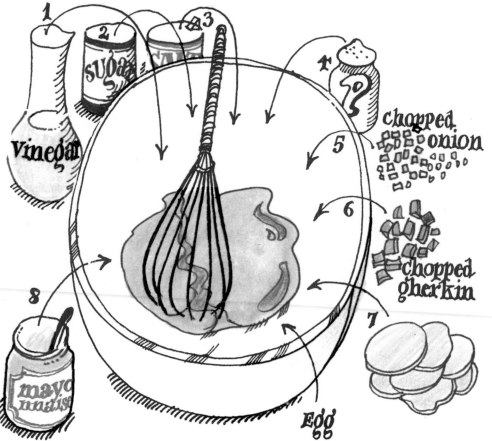

Kartoffel Salat

I always think of this salad as being distinctly German, and
this is an authentic German recipe. The taste is especially
fine with frankfurters, any cold meat, and, would you believe it,
fried fish. (You may find it even more to your liking than french fries.)
In Germany no picnic is complete without the potato salad.

1 small white cabbage, about 1 lb
salt and pepper to taste
½ teaspoon sugar
2 tablespoons vinegar
1 small green pepper, seeded and sliced (optional)
1 teaspoon celery seed (optional)
3 tablespoons good mayonnaise
chopped chives *or* parsley

(Serves 4–6)

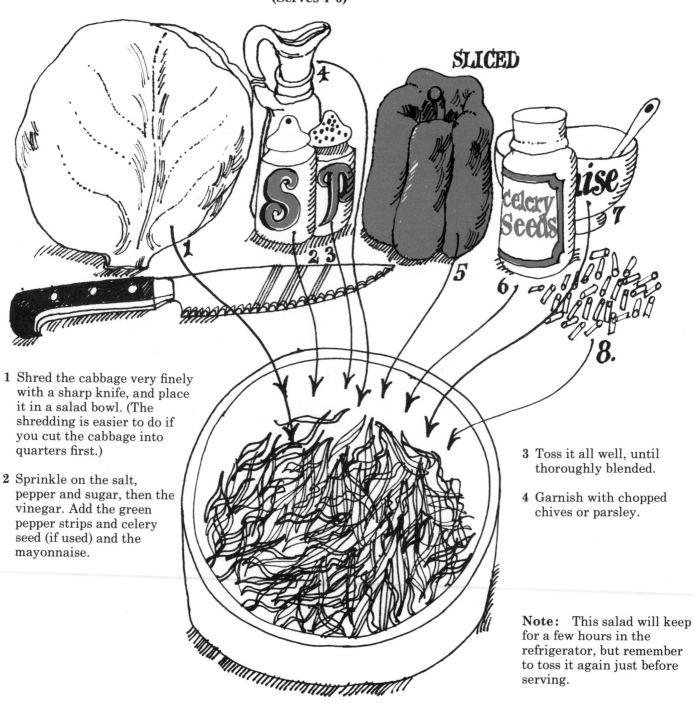

1 Shred the cabbage very finely with a sharp knife, and place it in a salad bowl. (The shredding is easier to do if you cut the cabbage into quarters first.)

2 Sprinkle on the salt, pepper and sugar, then the vinegar. Add the green pepper strips and celery seed (if used) and the mayonnaise.

3 Toss it all well, until thoroughly blended.

4 Garnish with chopped chives or parsley.

Note: This salad will keep for a few hours in the refrigerator, but remember to toss it again just before serving.

COLESLAW

Coleslaw is something I've
been eating as long as I can
remember. Especially popular
in Continental Europe and America.
Its creamy dressing makes it ideal as an
accompaniment to fish, french fries or hambur-
ger, or, for that matter, any fried meat.

77

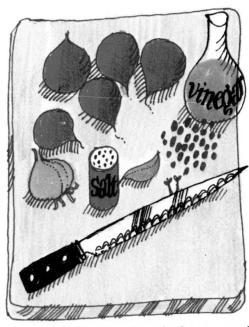

2 lb beetroot
1 large onion, cut into rings
$\frac{1}{2}$ cup vinegar
$\frac{1}{2}$ cup water
2 teaspoons sugar
1 bayleaf
4 peppercorns
2 whole cloves
$\frac{1}{2}$ teaspoon salt
$\frac{1}{2}$ teaspoon caraway seeds (optional)

(Serves 4)

1 Cook the beetroot in salted water until tender, peel them, and cut them into slices.

2 Place them in a deep china or glass dish together with the onion rings.

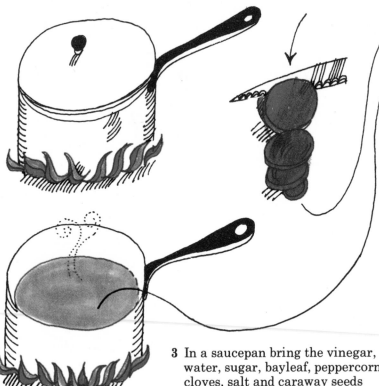

4 Leave to cool and then refrigerate until ready to use.

3 In a saucepan bring the vinegar, water, sugar, bayleaf, peppercorns, cloves, salt and caraway seeds to the boil. When it just reaches the boiling point, pour this marinade over the beetroot and onions.

Note: This salad will keep for about a week if tightly covered and kept in the refrigerator.

Beetroot Salad

This recipe was one of my grandmother's favorites. The marinade gives this salad its unique taste and distinctive, old-fashioned kind of flavor. Especially good with cold meats, fried fish and potato dishes. (In England the greengrocer always sells beetroot already boiled, which makes making this salad much easier; alas this is not the case in the States.)

For weight watchers – almost zero calories.

1 lb green string beans *or* **1 large can cut green beans**
3 tablespoons oil
1 tablespoon vinegar
salt and pepper to taste
1 small onion, finely chopped, *or* **shallot** *or* **3–4 spring onions**
½ teaspoon dried tarragon, oregano, dill *or* **garlic (optional)**
1 sprig of parsley for garnish

(Serves 4)

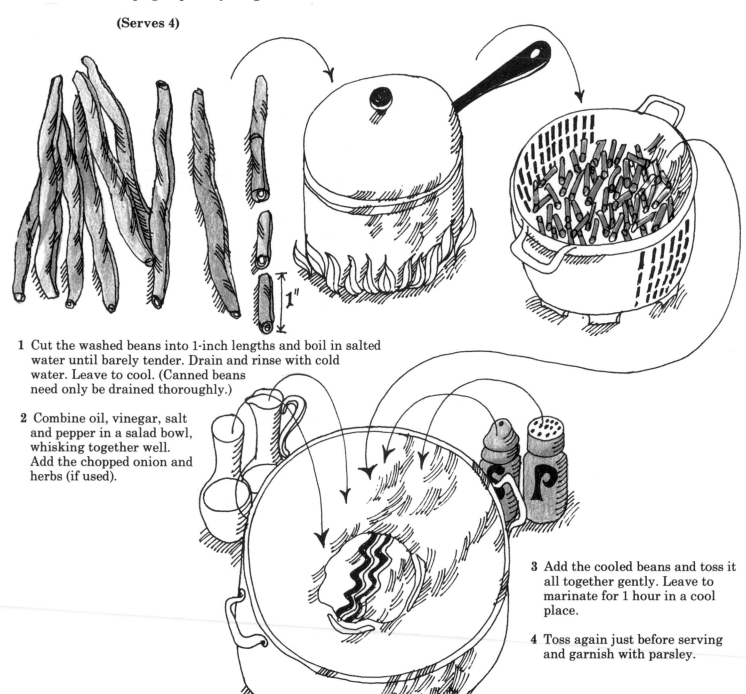

1 Cut the washed beans into 1-inch lengths and boil in salted water until barely tender. Drain and rinse with cold water. Leave to cool. (Canned beans need only be drained thoroughly.)

2 Combine oil, vinegar, salt and pepper in a salad bowl, whisking together well. Add the chopped onion and herbs (if used).

3 Add the cooled beans and toss it all together gently. Leave to marinate for 1 hour in a cool place.

4 Toss again just before serving and garnish with parsley.

Bohnensalat

An old German salad. This is my own recipe,
inherited from my mother, who inherited it
from her mother, who I suspect inherited it
from her mother. However, this particular recipe
I like to feel is distinguished by its simplicity.
Smooth and soft, it can be served instead of a vegetable
with just about any dish.

4 firm green peppers
1 clove garlic
¼ teaspoon salt
5 tablespoons olive oil
1 small tin pimientos
  or **add 1 red pepper to the green ones**
a few pitted black olives

(Serves 4)

1 To peel the peppers spear them on a
   fork and scorch the skin over a flame
   until it turns quite black, then
   scrape it off with a knife.

2 Cut the peeled peppers into
   quarters and remove all the seeds.
   Cut them into strips.

3 Crush the clove of garlic into the
   salt until it turns almost to a
   liquid, then with a wire whisk beat
   in the oil in a thin, steady stream.

4 Arrange the peppers attractively on a
   platter, scatter the pimientos (or the red
   pepper strips) over them, and pour the
   dressing over. Garnish with the olives.
   Cover the dish and leave the flavors to
   mingle for 30–60 minutes.

Note: This salad will keep for 2–3 days if
kept tightly covered in a refrigerator.

Pepper **Salad Provençale**

A truly magnificent French recipe, a Mediterranean delight. The grace and flavor of this salad complements almost any meal. Or alternatively it can be served as part of an hors d'oeuvre. You will find its taste smooth, soft, and unusually different.

½ lb firm green or white cabbage, thinly shredded
½ lb red cabbage, thinly shredded
salt and pepper to taste
1 green pepper, seeded and cut into strips (optional)
1 small onion, thinly sliced
4 tablespoons oil
2 tablespoons vinegar
1 tablespoon chopped parsley

(Serves 4–6)

1 Cut both cabbages into quarters and shred them very thinly with a sharp knife. Discard the core.

2 Place the shredded cabbage in a bowl, add the salt, pepper, green pepper strips and onion rings. Toss lightly.

3 In a screwtop jar combine oil and vinegar and shake until thoroughly blended.

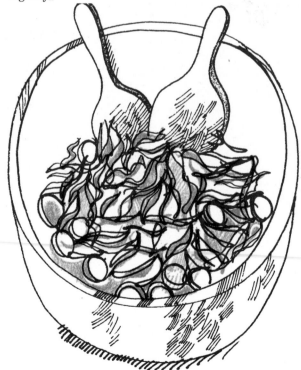

4 Pour the dressing over the salad, toss it thoroughly, and refrigerate until ready to use.

5 Just before serving toss it again lightly and sprinkle with the chopped parsley.

stimulating to the palate. It makes a fine winter salad.

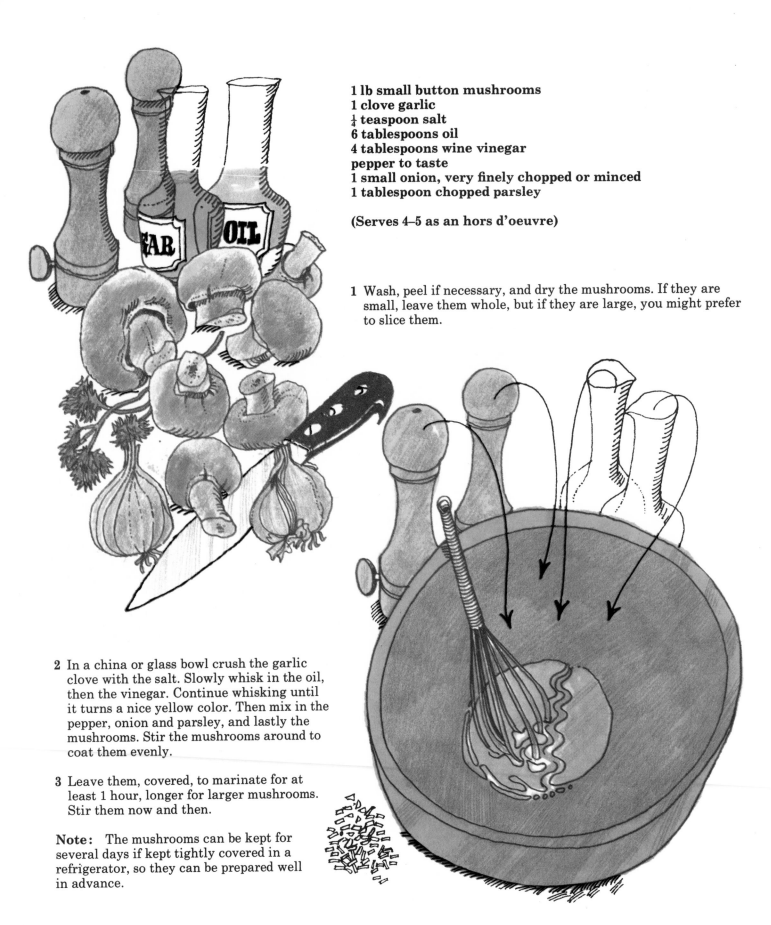

1 lb small button mushrooms
1 clove garlic
¼ teaspoon salt
6 tablespoons oil
4 tablespoons wine vinegar
pepper to taste
1 small onion, very finely chopped or minced
1 tablespoon chopped parsley

(Serves 4–5 as an hors d'oeuvre)

1 Wash, peel if necessary, and dry the mushrooms. If they are small, leave them whole, but if they are large, you might prefer to slice them.

2 In a china or glass bowl crush the garlic clove with the salt. Slowly whisk in the oil, then the vinegar. Continue whisking until it turns a nice yellow color. Then mix in the pepper, onion and parsley, and lastly the mushrooms. Stir the mushrooms around to coat them evenly.

3 Leave them, covered, to marinate for at least 1 hour, longer for larger mushrooms. Stir them now and then.

Note: The mushrooms can be kept for several days if kept tightly covered in a refrigerator, so they can be prepared well in advance.

Mushroom Salad

mushrooms to leave them soft and absolutely delicious. Mushroom
salad can be served as an hors d'oeuvre, or as part of a buffet.

1 small celeriac
1½ oz chopped walnuts
½ lb green grapes, seeds removed
1 small eating apple
juice of 1 lemon
4 tablespoons good mayonnaise
salt and pepper to taste
chives or parsley, chopped, for garnish

(Serves 4)

1 Boil the celeriac in salted water until tender; at least 30 minutes. Test as for potatoes.

2 Peel off the skin and cut into ½-inch cubes.

chopped walnuts.

Deseeded grapes.

Lemon Juice

3 Place the cubes in a salad bowl. Add the roughly chopped walnuts and the seeded grapes. Peel the apple and cut it into small pieces. Coat the apple pieces with lemon juice to prevent their discoloring. Add to the salad bowl.

4 Make up a dressing of the mayonnaise, leftover lemon juice, salt and pepper. Add the dressing to the salad, and toss it all together lightly but thoroughly.

5 Refrigerate until ready to use, then sprinkle on the chives or parsley.

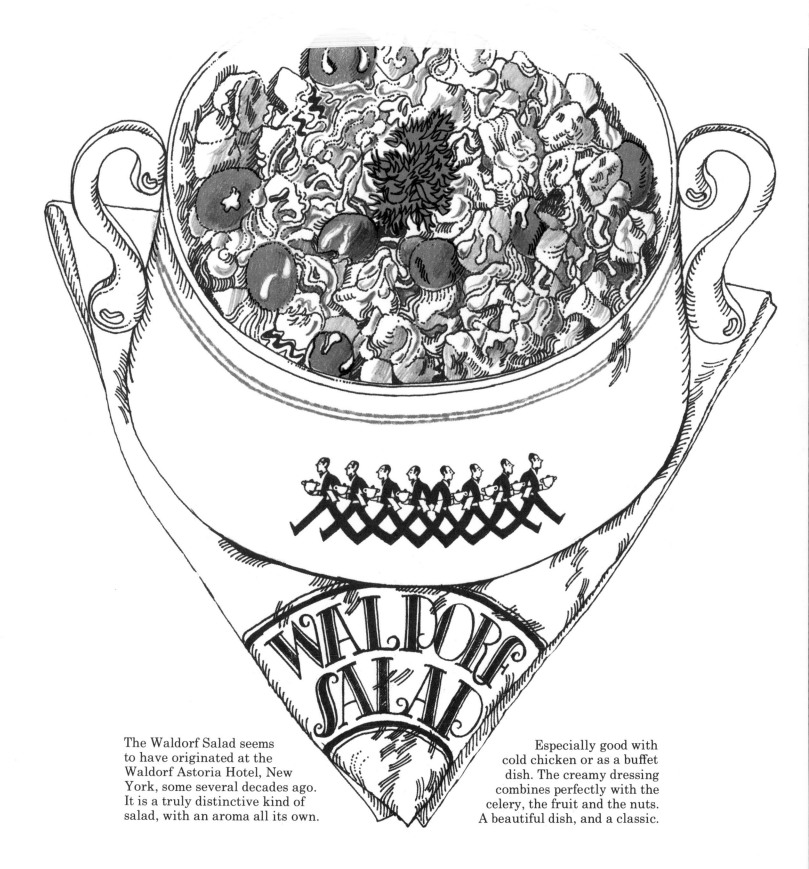

The Waldorf Salad seems to have originated at the Waldorf Astoria Hotel, New York, some several decades ago. It is a truly distinctive kind of salad, with an aroma all its own.

Especially good with cold chicken or as a buffet dish. The creamy dressing combines perfectly with the celery, the fruit and the nuts. A beautiful dish, and a classic.

2 lettuce hearts
2 cans tuna fish
10 or so pitted black olives
1 onion, cut into rings
2 tomatoes, cut into wedges
¼ lb or more cooked string beans
1 green pepper, cut into strips
1 hardboiled egg, cut into wedges
½ cup olive oil
4 tablespoons white wine vinegar
¼ teaspoon dried tarragon
¼ teaspoon dried dill
salt and pepper to taste
1 clove garlic, crushed

(Serves 4 for lunch or 6 as an hors d'oeuvre)

1 Wash and dry the lettuce and tear it into bite-size pieces. Line a nice platter with them.

2 Mound the tuna fish in the centre and garnish the platter attractively with olives, onion rings, tomatoes, string beans, pepper strips and wedges of hard-boiled egg.

3 Make a vinaigrette dressing from the rest of the ingredients in a screw top jar or bottle, and shake it to combine it all thoroughly.

4 Pour the dressing over the salad and serve immediately.

Note: Niçoise salad lends itself to great variations. Sometimes it can also include boiled and cubed potato, anchovy fillets, cooked artichoke bottoms or peas.

90

...igorating in July. A truly great salad that is a ... complete meal in itself.

...It can also be served as an hors d'oeuvre.

1 large head of romaine
3–4 slices white bread
enough oil to fry the bread
salt and pepper to taste
5 tablespoons olive oil
1 clove garlic, crushed
1 egg, boiled for 10 seconds only
3 tablespoons white wine vinegar
4 tablespoons grated Parmesan
5 chopped anchovy fillets (optional)

(Serves 4)

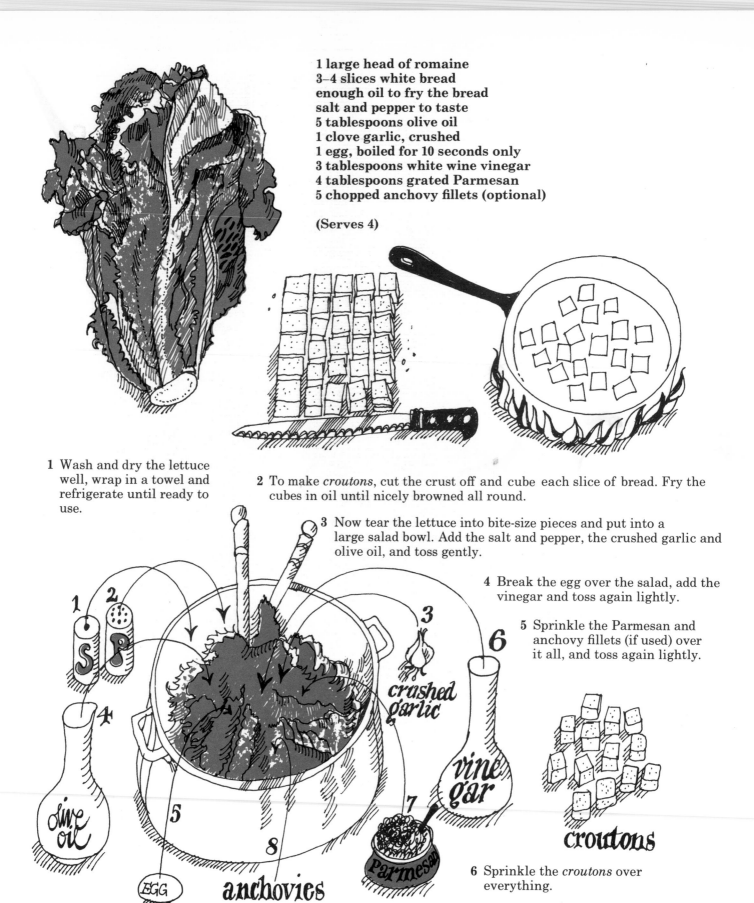

1 Wash and dry the lettuce well, wrap in a towel and refrigerate until ready to use.

2 To make *croutons*, cut the crust off and cube each slice of bread. Fry the cubes in oil until nicely browned all round.

3 Now tear the lettuce into bite-size pieces and put into a large salad bowl. Add the salt and pepper, the crushed garlic and olive oil, and toss gently.

4 Break the egg over the salad, add the vinegar and toss again lightly.

5 Sprinkle the Parmesan and anchovy fillets (if used) over it all, and toss again lightly.

6 Sprinkle the *croutons* over everything.

Serve immediately.

Caesar Salad

A Southern California classic. The rich tender greens make a particularly crisp salad. The fresh flavor of the dressing makes it a highly distinctive dish for the connoisseur or novice alike. There are numerous variations of the Caesar Salad, but to my own knowledge this recipe is the most authentic.

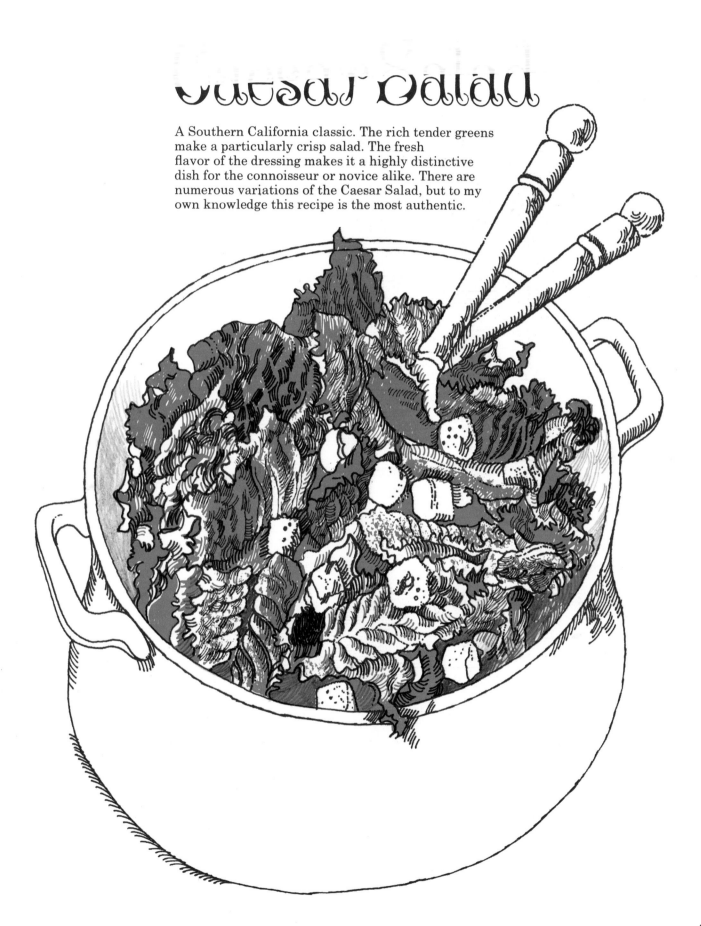

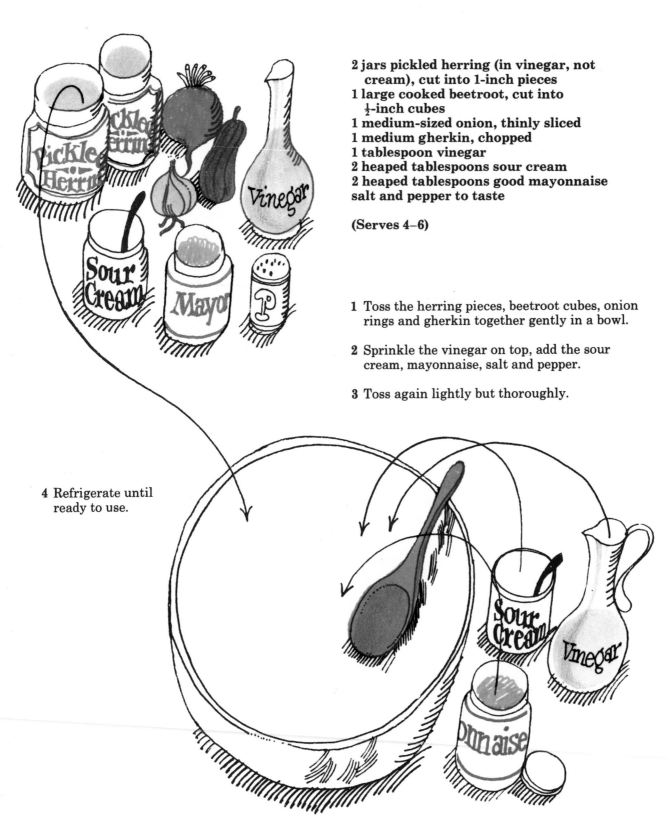

2 jars pickled herring (in vinegar, not
   cream), cut into 1-inch pieces
1 large cooked beetroot, cut into
   $\frac{1}{2}$-inch cubes
1 medium-sized onion, thinly sliced
1 medium gherkin, chopped
1 tablespoon vinegar
2 heaped tablespoons sour cream
2 heaped tablespoons good mayonnaise
salt and pepper to taste

(Serves 4–6)

1 Toss the herring pieces, beetroot cubes, onion
  rings and gherkin together gently in a bowl.

2 Sprinkle the vinegar on top, add the sour
  cream, mayonnaise, salt and pepper.

3 Toss again lightly but thoroughly.

4 Refrigerate until
  ready to use.

Note: This salad will keep for a day or two if tightly covered and kept in a refrigerator.

Hering Salat

A simple version of an authentic German recipe. Creamy, fishy, and beautifully smooth. It makes an ideal hors d'oeuvre or buffet dish. Or, as a midnight snack after a late night out, it will help to clear your head the morning after.

1 onion, thinly sliced
1 orange, cut into segments
4 tablespoons oil
4 tablespoons vinegar
salt and pepper to taste
1 head lettuce (any kind)

(Serves 4)

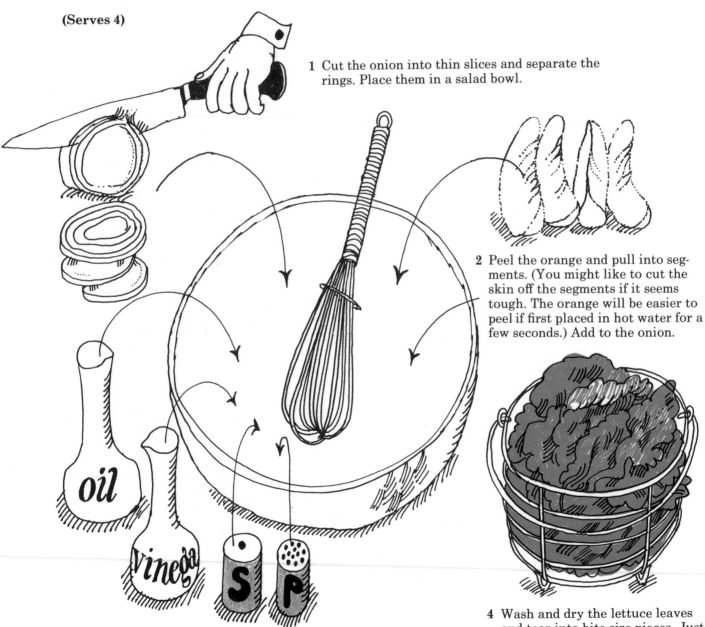

1 Cut the onion into thin slices and separate the rings. Place them in a salad bowl.

2 Peel the orange and pull into segments. (You might like to cut the skin off the segments if it seems tough. The orange will be easier to peel if first placed in hot water for a few seconds.) Add to the onion.

3 Combine the oil, vinegar, salt and pepper, and whisk until well blended. Pour this mixture over the onions and orange. Cover the bowl and leave to marinate in the refrigerator for 1 hour.

4 Wash and dry the lettuce leaves and tear into bite-size pieces. Just before serving, gently toss the lettuce in the marinade.

Serve immediately.

Spanish Salad

The orange and onion give this salad a really delightful flavour. Crisp, juicy and truly refreshing, it is a salad that can be enjoyed at any time of the year.

The combination of flavours goes well with light meat, chicken or fish.

1 head lettuce (preferably Iceberg)
½ lb cold, cooked chicken, cubed
¼ lb thick sliced ham, cubed
¼ lb cheese, cubed (any kind)
2 hardboiled eggs, cut into wedges
2 tomatoes, cut into wedges
1 bunch watercress
5 spring onions
a Salad Dressing *or* the
vinaigrette dressing for Salad Niçoise.

(Serves 4)

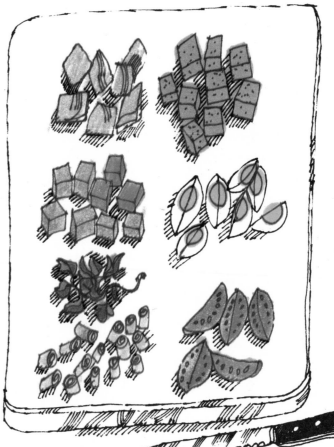

1 Wash and dry all the vegetables. Tear the lettuce into bite-size pieces, and place in a wide, shallow bowl or on a platter.

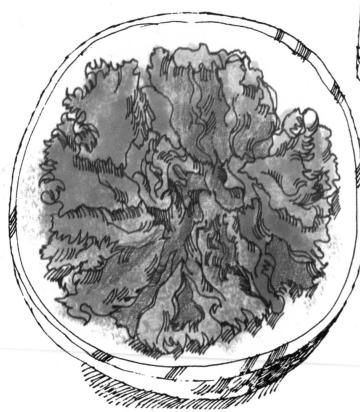

2 On top of the lettuce arrange the chicken cubes, ham cubes, cheese cubes, egg wedges, tomato wedges, watercress and spring onions in an attractive pattern.

3 Pass the dressing separately in a small bowl. Let everyone help themselves to the salad first, and then let them pour their own desired amount of dressing.

...salad makes an ideal light lunch or supper. Try it with a glass of wine and a chunk of crusty bread. Especially fine on a hot summer's day. Its wholesome goodness also makes it a fine picnic salad.

enough raw spinach for your needs
1 small cucumber
salt
2 tablespoons red wine vinegar
4 tablespoons oil
salt and pepper to taste
a little dry mustard

(Serves 4)

1 Wash the spinach well and clean it of any tough leaves and stems. Leave to dry completely.

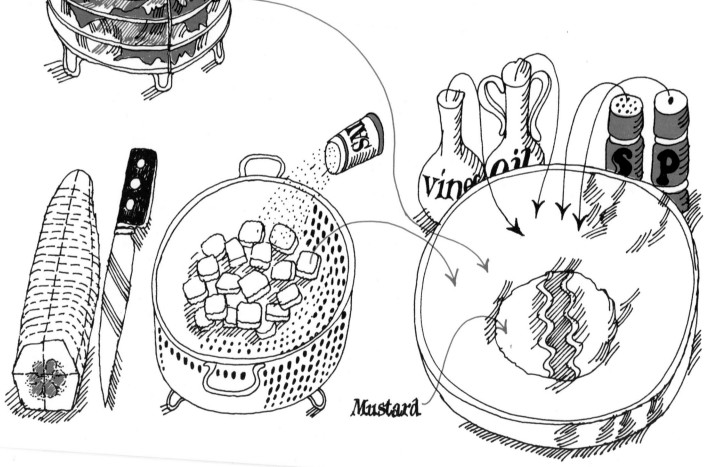

2 Peel the cucumber and cut into small cubes and place them in a colander. Sprinkle on some salt and leave to drain for at least 30 minutes. Rinse with cold water and leave them to dry.

3 Mix the vinegar, oil, salt, pepper and dry mustard together in a salad bowl, add the spinach and the cucumber, and toss together gently but thoroughly.

Serve immediately.

SALAD SPINACH SALAD DAYS

A salad of good, earthy character, honest and sincere. The combination of spinach and velvety cucumber, plus the dressing, gives this salad a distinctive taste all its own. Zesty, robust and highly nutritious.

Mothers might be interested to know that this is the only way I can get my children to eat spinach. An unusual accompaniment to any main course.

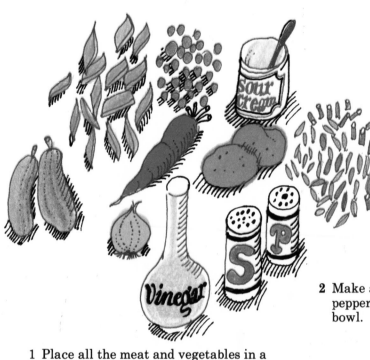

½–¾ lb lean, cooked, cold meat
    (leftover veal, beef, pork or lamb, cut into
    julienne strips about 1 inch long
    and ¼ inch wide)
1 cup cooked green peas
1 large carrot, cooked and cubed
2 cold, boiled potatoes, cubed
2 gherkins, cubed
1 medium onion, cut into julienne strips
2 tablespoons vinegar
3–4 tablespoons juice from gherkins
salt and pepper to taste
1 level teaspoon sugar
1 small carton sour cream
chopped parsley or chives for garnish

(Serves 4–6)

2 Make a marinade of vinegar, gherkin juice, salt and
pepper and the sugar, and pour it over the salad in the
bowl.

3 Leave to marinate in the refrigerator for an hour or
longer, tossing it once in a while.

1 Place all the meat and vegetables in a
salad bowl.

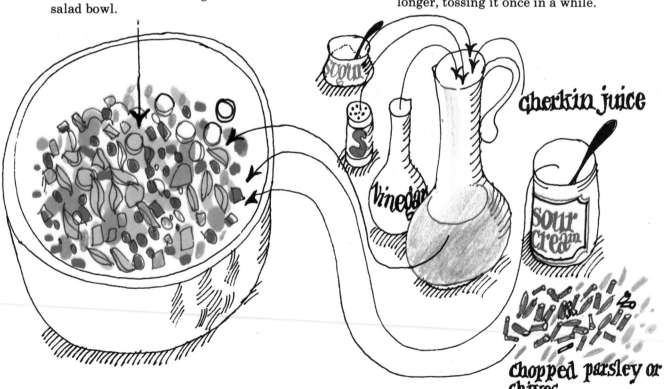

4 Then fold in gently but
thoroughly the sour cream.

5 Dust with chopped parsley or
chives.

Note: This salad will keep for a day or two if tightly covered
and kept in a refrigerator.
    You can also use cooked green beans, broad beans, capers,
black or green olives, cooked beetroot or cooked mushrooms.

RUSSIAN SALAD

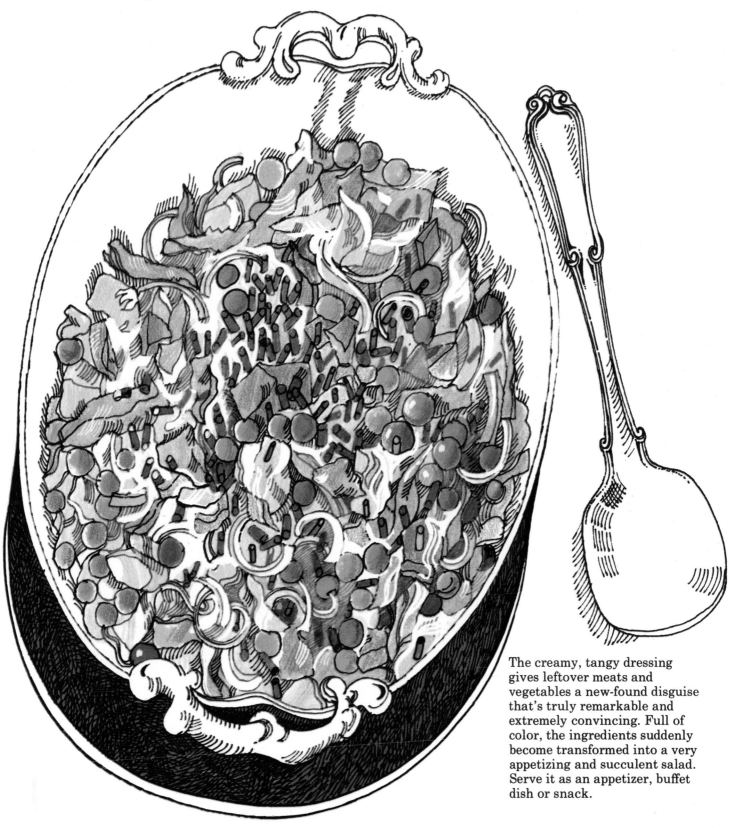

The creamy, tangy dressing gives leftover meats and vegetables a new-found disguise that's truly remarkable and extremely convincing. Full of color, the ingredients suddenly become transformed into a very appetizing and succulent salad. Serve it as an appetizer, buffet dish or snack.

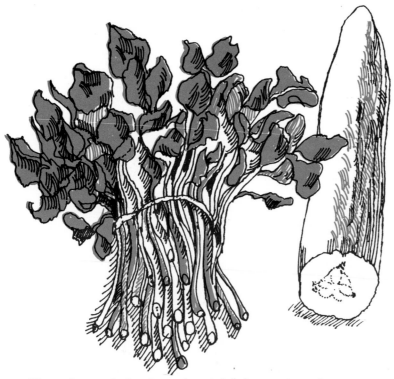

2 bunches watercress
½ cucumber, peeled and thinly sliced
4 oz blue cheese, crumbled (optional)
3 tablespoons fresh lemon juice
8 tablespoons oil
salt and pepper to taste

(Serves 4)

1 Place the washed, trimmed and dried watercress in a salad bowl, add the sliced cucumber and the crumbled cheese (if used).

2 Toss it all together.

3 Into a screwtop jar put the lemon juice, oil, salt and pepper, and shake it well until thoroughly mixed and thick and creamy.

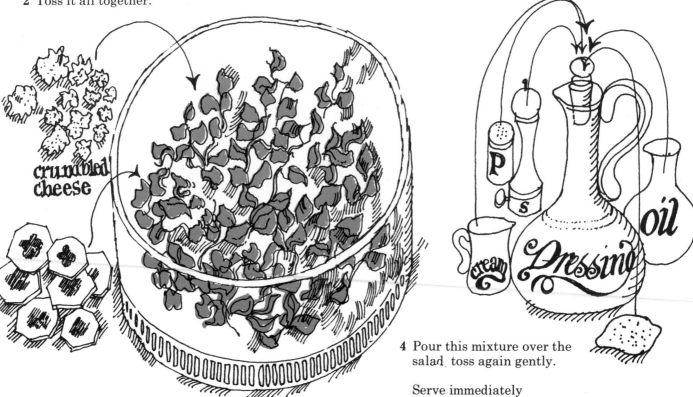

crumbled cheese

4 Pour this mixture over the salad, toss again gently.

Serve immediately

Watercress Salad

You could call this a real English salad, insofar as watercress must be more readily available in England than anywhere else. The tangy lemon dressing gives this salad a delicate taste. Ideal as an accompaniment to any main course.

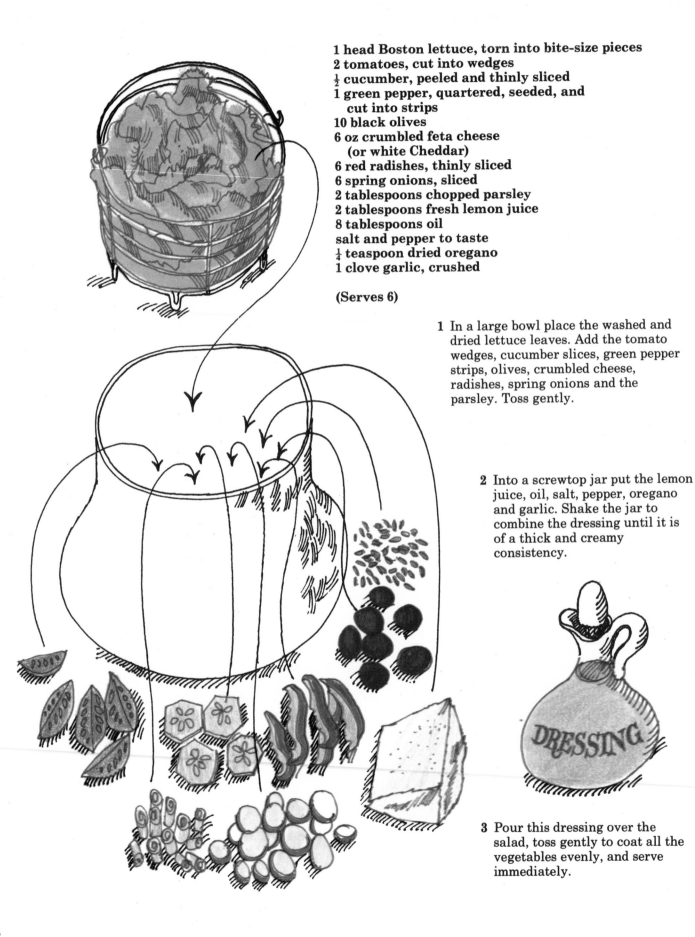

1 head Boston lettuce, torn into bite-size pieces
2 tomatoes, cut into wedges
½ cucumber, peeled and thinly sliced
1 green pepper, quartered, seeded, and
  cut into strips
10 black olives
6 oz crumbled feta cheese
  (or white Cheddar)
6 red radishes, thinly sliced
6 spring onions, sliced
2 tablespoons chopped parsley
2 tablespoons fresh lemon juice
8 tablespoons oil
salt and pepper to taste
¼ teaspoon dried oregano
1 clove garlic, crushed

(Serves 6)

1 In a large bowl place the washed and dried lettuce leaves. Add the tomato wedges, cucumber slices, green pepper strips, olives, crumbled cheese, radishes, spring onions and the parsley. Toss gently.

2 Into a screwtop jar put the lemon juice, oil, salt, pepper, oregano and garlic. Shake the jar to combine the dressing until it is of a thick and creamy consistency.

DRESSING

3 Pour this dressing over the salad, toss gently to coat all the vegetables evenly, and serve immediately.

greek salad

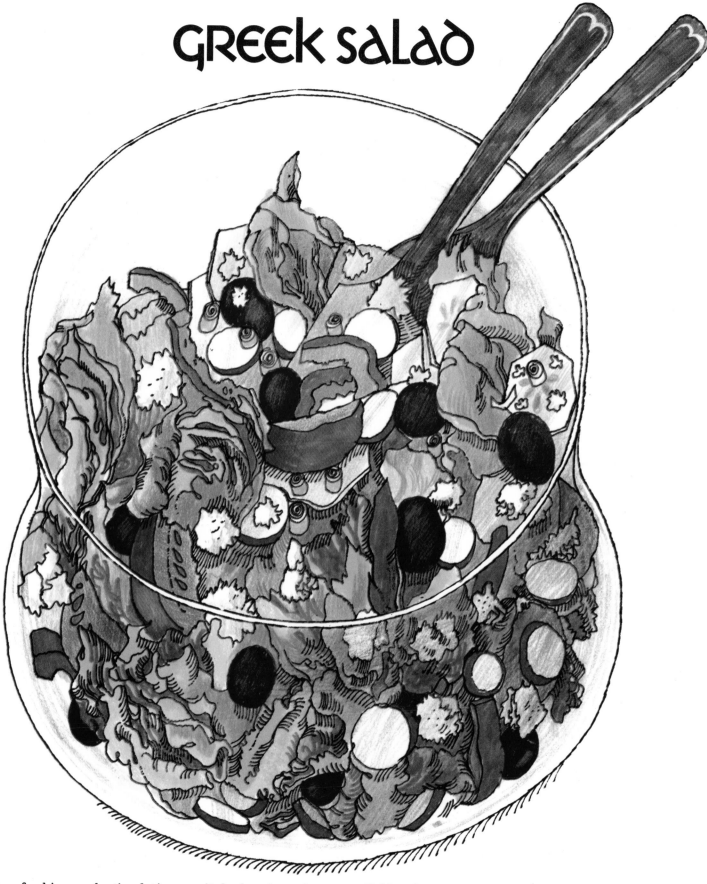

As refreshing and stimulating as it looks. A perfect blend of vegetables and cheese. The lemon dressing gives it a good tangy taste. The feta cheese gives an authentic Mediterranean flavor. However, if feta cheese is not available, do not despair, white Cheddar makes an adequate substitute.

Excellent as a first course or as a side dish. A favorite in our household.

½ lb thick sliced bacon
oil for frying bacon
6 heads endive
2 hardboiled eggs, chopped
8 tablespoons oil
2 tablespoons vinegar
salt and pepper to taste
2 tablespoons chopped parsley

(Serves 4–6)

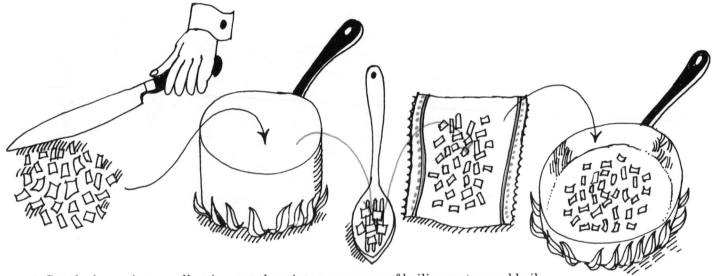

1 Cut the bacon into small strips, put them into a saucepan of boiling water, and boil
them for 10 minutes to reduce the saltiness. Remove them with a slotted spoon
and dry them on a paper towel. When thoroughly dry, fry the strips in the oil in a
frying pan until crisp.

chopped egg

2 Cut the endive into
½-inch, thick slices
and place them in a
salad bowl. Add the
chopped egg.

3 Make up the dressing
of oil, vinegar, salt and
pepper. Pour this
mixture over the salad
and toss it together
gently but thoroughly.

4 Place it on a nice platter
and sprinkle the bacon bits
and parsley on top.

Serve very soon.

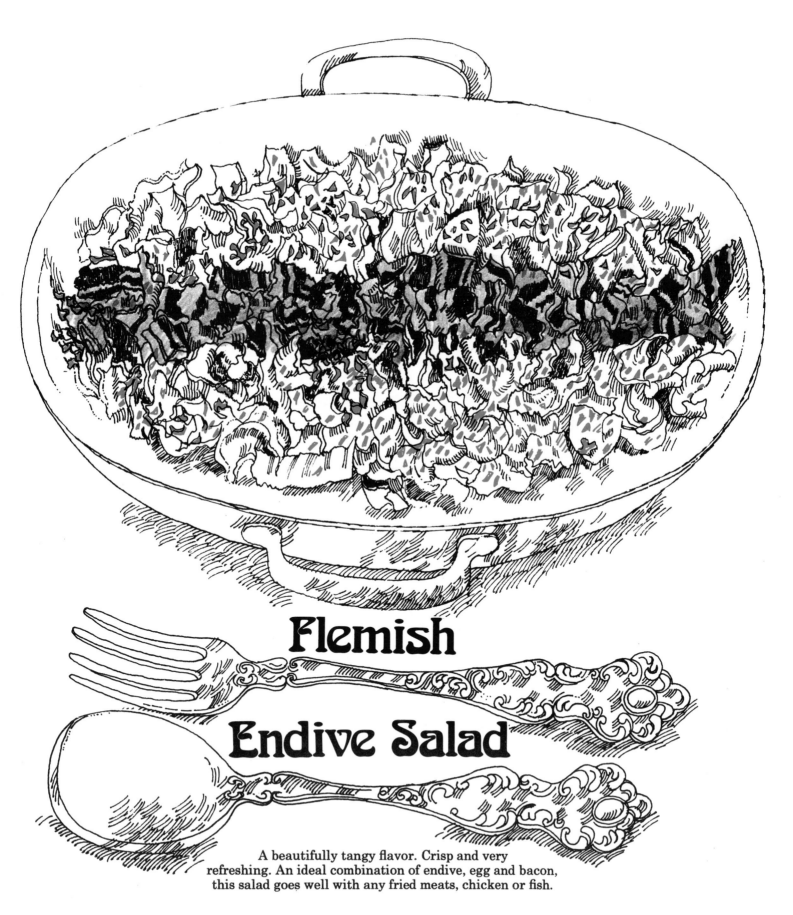

Flemish
Endive Salad

A beautifully tangy flavor. Crisp and very
refreshing. An ideal combination of endive, egg and bacon,
this salad goes well with any fried meats, chicken or fish.

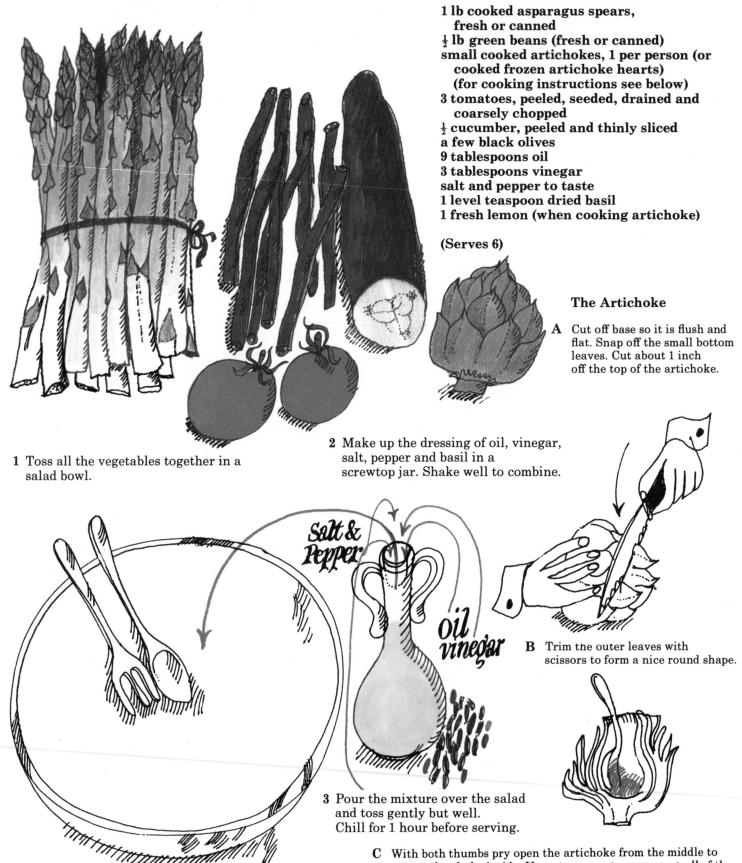

1 lb cooked asparagus spears,
   fresh or canned
½ lb green beans (fresh or canned)
small cooked artichokes, 1 per person (or
   cooked frozen artichoke hearts)
   (for cooking instructions see below)
3 tomatoes, peeled, seeded, drained and
   coarsely chopped
½ cucumber, peeled and thinly sliced
a few black olives
9 tablespoons oil
3 tablespoons vinegar
salt and pepper to taste
1 level teaspoon dried basil
1 fresh lemon (when cooking artichoke)

(Serves 6)

The Artichoke

A Cut off base so it is flush and
flat. Snap off the small bottom
leaves. Cut about 1 inch
off the top of the artichoke.

1 Toss all the vegetables together in a
salad bowl.

2 Make up the dressing of oil, vinegar,
salt, pepper and basil in a
screwtop jar. Shake well to combine.

Salt & Pepper

oil vinegar

B Trim the outer leaves with
scissors to form a nice round shape.

3 Pour the mixture over the salad
and toss gently but well.
Chill for 1 hour before serving.

4 Toss again lightly, decorate with olives and serve
from the salad bowl or transfer it to a platter.

C With both thumbs pry open the artichoke from the middle to
expose the choke inside. Use a teaspoon to scrape out *all* of the
hairy choke, and push the artichoke back into shape. Brush
with lemon juice to prevent it discoloring and boil in salted
water for 15 minutes. Drain and leave to cool before using.

Italian Summer Salad

A real Italian salad. A typically Mediterranean combination. This is truly a magnificent recipe, grand enough to stand as an elegant starter. Or it can make an unusual side dish to the main course.

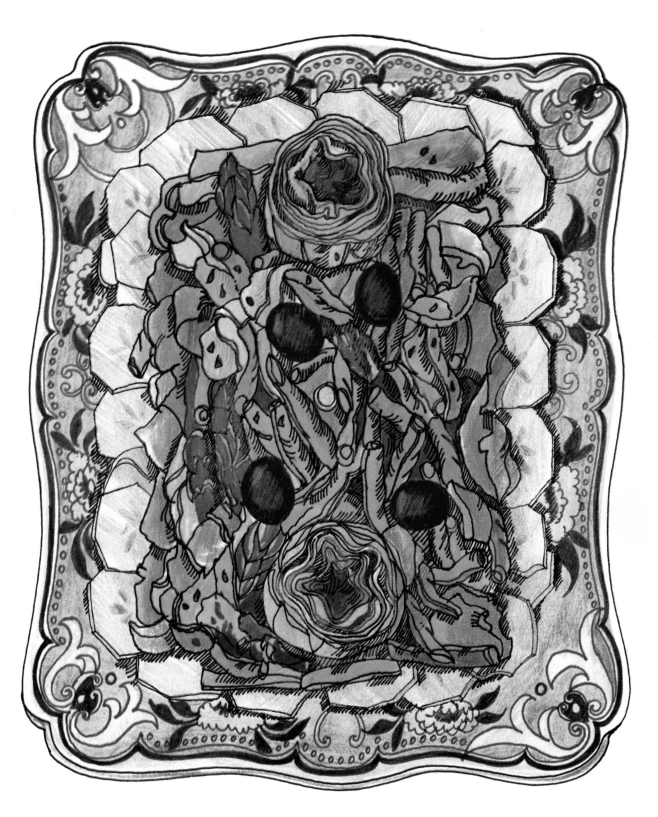

1 can salmon
2 heaped tablespoons very finely chopped
  celery
2 hardboiled eggs, chopped
4 tablespoons good mayonnaise
½ teaspoon curry powder

2 avocados
juice of 1 lemon
some nice lettuce leaves
paprika for garnish

(Serves 4)

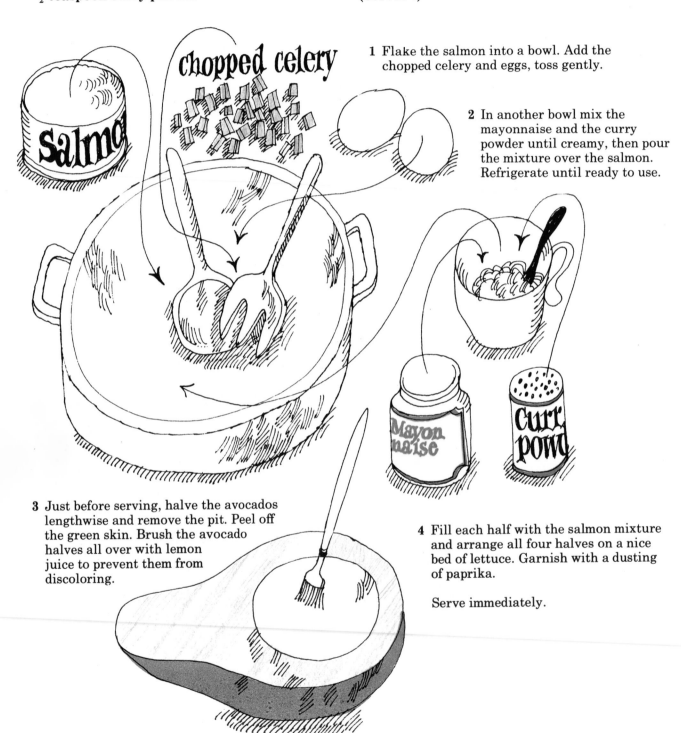

chopped celery

salmon

Mayonnaise

Curry powder

1 Flake the salmon into a bowl. Add the chopped celery and eggs, toss gently.

2 In another bowl mix the mayonnaise and the curry powder until creamy, then pour the mixture over the salmon. Refrigerate until ready to use.

3 Just before serving, halve the avocados lengthwise and remove the pit. Peel off the green skin. Brush the avocado halves all over with lemon juice to prevent them from discoloring.

4 Fill each half with the salmon mixture and arrange all four halves on a nice bed of lettuce. Garnish with a dusting of paprika.

Serve immediately.

Salmon & Avocado Salad

This makes an excellent hors d'oeuvre, winter and summer alike.
The smooth taste of the avocado blends ideally with the texture of
the salmon, eggs and celery. Very attractive to the eye.

1 small cucumber
¼ cup plus 2 tablespoons oil
5 tablespoons white wine vinegar
1 clove garlic, crushed
1 teaspoon dried basil
salt and pepper to taste
½ lb button mushrooms
5 spring onions, chopped
2 tablespoons chopped parsley
3 tomatoes, cut into wedges
1 green pepper, quartered, seeded and
   cut into strips

(Serves 4)

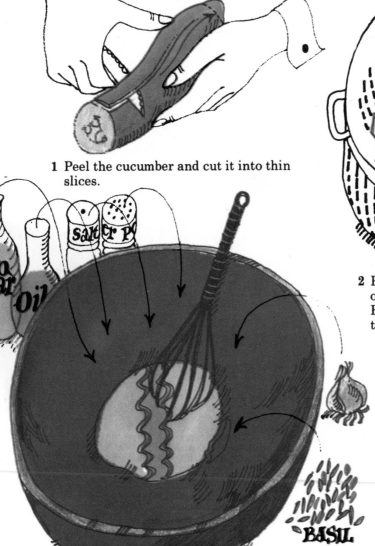

1 Peel the cucumber and cut it into thin slices.

2 Place them in a colander, sprinkle some salt on top and leave to drain for 30 minutes. Rinse them with cold water and dry thoroughly.

3 In a large bowl make the dressing by combining the oil, vinegar, garlic, basil, salt and pepper thoroughly.

4 Add the whole mushrooms and chopped spring onions, the drained cucumber slices and the parsley, and toss all together gently. Chill in the refrigerator for an hour or more.

5 Place the tomato wedges over the salad in the bowl and over them the green pepper strips. Toss all the vegetables gently but thoroughly.

Serve immediately.

A super salad when served really fresh and slightly chilled. Juicy and refreshing. An ideal side dish to accompany any meat course.

1 head lettuce (any kind)
6 red radishes, cut into slices
2 tomatoes, cut into slices
2 celery stalks, chopped
½ cucumber, peeled and diced
6 stuffed green olives, sliced
1 bunch watercress, trimmed
½ lb cooked shrimp
  (fresh or frozen)
8 tablespoons oil

4 tablespoons vinegar
salt and pepper to taste
1 teaspoon dried tarragon
1 green pepper, cut into rings and seeded

(Serves 4–6)

1 Wash and dry the lettuce leaves and tear them into
  bite-size pieces. Place them in a salad bowl.

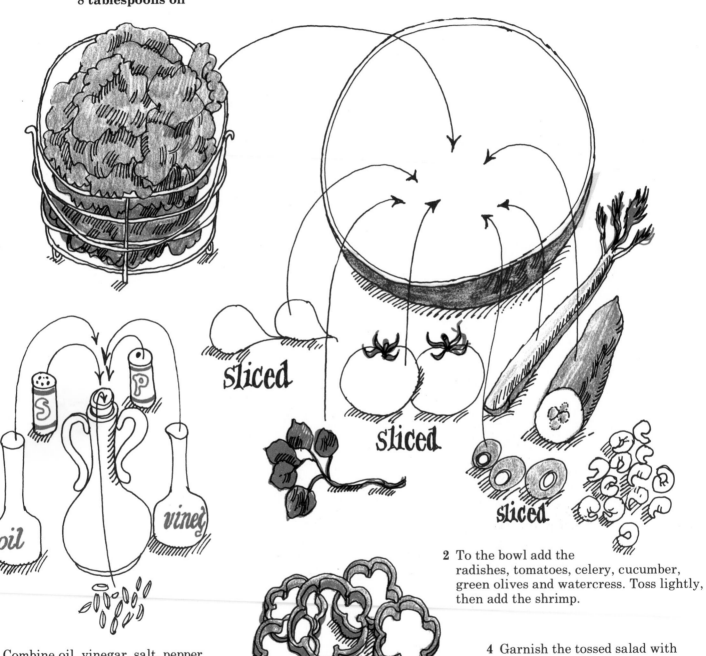

2 To the bowl add the
  radishes, tomatoes, celery, cucumber,
  green olives and watercress. Toss lightly,
  then add the shrimp.

3 Combine oil, vinegar, salt, pepper
  and tarragon in a screwtop jar, and
  shake well to combine. Pour it over
  the salad and toss well.

4 Garnish the tossed salad with
  the green pepper rings.

  Serve immediately.

sliced

sliced

sliced

oil

vineg

116

Shrimp Salad

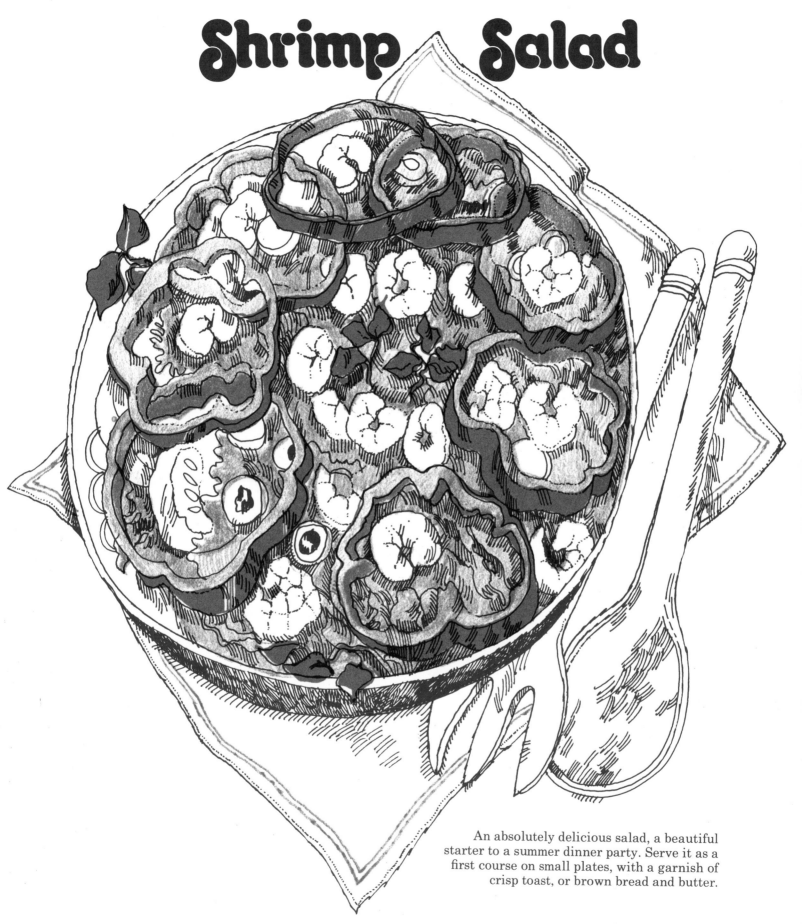

An absolutely delicious salad, a beautiful starter to a summer dinner party. Serve it as a first course on small plates, with a garnish of crisp toast, or brown bread and butter.

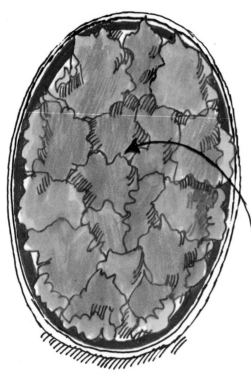

1 head lettuce
1 can crabmeat *or* ½ lb frozen crabmeat, cooked
6 heaped tablespoons good mayonnaise
4 tablespoons heavy cream
2 level teaspoons paprika
1 teaspoon Worcestershire sauce
5 spring onions, chopped
2 tablespoons fresh lemon juice
salt and pepper to taste
2 hardboiled eggs, cut into wedges
lemon wedges
1 tablespoon chopped parsley

(Serves 2 for lunch and 4 as an hors d'oeuvre)

crabmeat

1 Arrange some perfect large lettuce leaves on a nice platter. Scatter the smaller leaves over them, or tear them into bite-size pieces.

2 Place the crabmeat in the centre of the platter and pour over it the following famous Louis dressing:

3 In a small bowl gently mix the mayonnaise, cream, paprika, Worcestershire sauce, spring onions, lemon juice, salt and pepper until well blended.

4 Garnish with wedges of hardboiled egg and lemon and sprinkle with parsley.

Serve immediately.

CRAB SALAD LOUIS

A San Francisco classic, this salad has endeared itself to millions of Americans. The special dressing together with the crab meat gives this salad a typically San Francisco flavor. It can be served as a first course or as a delightful summer lunch. Fresh and satisfying, the flavor more than justifies the additional cost of preparing this salad.

SALAD DRESSINGS

Mayonnaise

1 egg yolk
¼ teaspoon dry mustard
salt and pepper to taste
pinch of sugar
2 tablespoons wine vinegar
¼ cup plus 2 tablespoons oil

Place the egg yolk, mustard, salt, pepper and sugar in a deep bowl. Mix until well combined. Add the vinegar and whisk it (with a wooden spoon or wire whisk) until white and frothy. Add the oil slowly, drop by drop, whisking constantly, until all the oil is used.
Occasionally the mayonnaise will curdle. Start again in another bowl with just one egg yolk. Whisk it constantly and slowly and add the curdled mayonnaise to it, by the teaspoonful, until it is all smooth and creamy. If the mayonnaise seems too thick for your needs, thin it down with a little cream. Mayonnaise can also be made in a blender. (Follow the directions in your blender book.) Mayonnaise made in a blender does not have the same shine and texture.

Green Goddess Dressing

1 recipe mayonnaise as above
3 chopped anchovy fillets
3 spring onions, chopped
2 tablespoons chopped parsley
1 teaspoon dried tarragon
1 heaped tablespoon chopped chives
2 tablespoons wine vinegar

Mix all the ingredients until smooth and creamy. Refrigerate before using on any green salad.

Thousand Island Dressing

1 recipe mayonnaise as above
5 tablespoons ketchup
8 stuffed olives, finely chopped
1 small green pepper, finely chopped
1 tablespoon finely chopped chives or onion
1 hardboiled egg, chopped
1 tablespoon chopped parsley

Mix all the ingredients together until smooth and creamy. Refrigerate before using on any green salad.

Yogurt Dressing

1 carton yogurt (8 oz)
1 small clove garlic, crushed
½ teaspoon dried oregano
1 tablespoon oil
salt and pepper to taste
1 fresh lemon (juice only)

Mix well, until smooth, the yogurt, crushed garlic, oregano, oil, salt and pepper. Then stir in the lemon juice and blend until smooth and creamy. (About 280 calories.)

Creamy French Dressing

1 tablespoon paprika
1 teaspoon sugar
1 teaspoon salt
6 tablespoons vinegar
1 raw egg
½ cup plus 2 tablespoons oil

Combine paprika, sugar and salt. Add the vinegar and the egg and beat well. Add the oil in a slow stream, beating all the time, until the mixture is thick and creamy. Chill before serving over any green salad.

Blue Cheese Dressing

1 clove garlic
4 oz blue cheese
2 teaspoons Worcestershire sauce
juice of 1 lemon
½ teaspoon dry mustard
¼ teaspoon paprika
1 tablespoon oil
salt and pepper to taste
1 recipe mayonnaise as above

Mash garlic and cheese in a bowl. Add the Worcestershire sauce, lemon juice, mustard, paprika, oil, salt and pepper. Blend well. Add the mayonnaise and stir until smooth and creamy. Refrigerate before using over any green salad.

Watercress Dressing

2 tablespoons fresh lemon juice
1 tablespoon wine vinegar
½ teaspoon dried tarragon
¼ cup plus 2 tablespoons oil
salt and pepper to taste
1 bunch watercress

Mix lemon juice, vinegar, tarragon, oil, salt and pepper until well blended. Then stir in 1 bunch of finely chopped watercress. Use over any green salad.

Low Calorie Dressing

8 oz cottage cheese
¼ cup plus 2 tablespoons milk
salt and pepper to taste
2 tablespoons fresh lemon juice
1 small green pepper, chopped
5 spring onions, chopped
1 clove garlic, crushed

You can best do this in a blender. Just swirl all the ingredients around until well blended. Refrigerate before using on any green salad.
If a blender is not available, force the cottage cheese through a fine sieve, and add all the other ingredients to it. Blend until smooth. (About 350 calories.)

PASTA CONTENTS

Introduction

Pasta. From where did it come?

The origin of pasta has long since been lost in the mists of antiquity. The myth that pasta was introduced into Italy by Marco Polo does indeed seem mostly myth. For there appears to be a noticeable absence of any evidence to suggest that it might be historical fact. More credible is the theory that pasta was eaten by the Romans some considerable time before Marco Polo's travels to China.

Certainly the evolution of pasta has been typically Italian. Where else could such a basic staple as pasta have found expression in so many different forms and variations? Many have magnificently sculptured shapes, like miniature works of art, all touched by the Italian genius for recognizing no separation between art and life.

Such a complex heritage may explain why there are so many misconceptions surrounding the cooking and serving of pasta, all doing a gross injustice to the gastronomic feats and delights of Italian pasta cookery. Many people believe that pasta amounts to nothing much more than spaghetti, macaroni, ravioli and something they serve in the local Italian restaurant, called lasagne. Alas, what masquerades as a pasta dish in many so-called Italian restaurants is at the very best a pale imitation of the real thing.

It is sad that pasta cooking with its multifarious tastes and nutritional values has been too often carelessly practised. For pasta is a subtle, immensely versatile food, that is also satisfying, inexpensive, easy to prepare and, contrary to popular belief, low in calories. Low in calories in-so-far as a little pasta goes a long way, leaving the stomach feeling full and contented for hours.

For the Italians, pasta is not so much a meal as a way of life, such is their passion for pasta with its many colorful and regional variations. The joys of pasta can be as complex or as simple as you like – many Italians treasure as simple a dish of pasta as spaghetti tossed in olive oil with a grating of black pepper.

Should you wish to venture deep into the gourmet delights of pasta, try making your own dough from scratch. Homemade pasta may sound like a near impossibility – rest assured, it is not. It can be mastered very quickly for it requires no special skills – only patience and a little practice. Once mastered, the results can be most gratifying. Exquisite homemade ravioli with a filling of juicy, delicately flavored meat or aromatic cheeses. Or cannelloni, stuffed with a succulent beef-and-spinach filling. Or tortellini with a characteristically Italian filling of ricotta cheese.

There are also the delights of regional sauces with their pungent flavors of herbs and spices, such as Genoese pesto, with its flavoring of fresh basil (it is worth giving up a little corner of your garden to grow it) and the ever-famous and versatile bolognese sauce.

In this book you will find a collection of traditional recipes with the flavor and sumptuous delight of Italian cooking. In selecting the recipes an attempt has been made to balance the many regional flavors of Italian cooking, using only the traditional ingredients – although you may find it necessary to compromise from time to time. Taking into account the availability of certain ingredients I have indicated alternatives when they might seem necessary.

The design of this book we hope reflects our love of pasta. For selecting the recipes and preparing the drawings have been an absolute delight, to which our stomachs can well testify. Our Look and Cook format has been devised for ease of use and understanding, so that at a glance the reader can comprehend how a dish is prepared and how, finally, it should look when it reaches the dinner table.

As a footnote to this introduction, we would like to express our grateful thanks and appreciation to our publishers for their kindness in allowing us to produce this book. We are also indebted to many friends who have offered suggestions in the preparation of the manuscript – in particular our old friends Carla and Frankie Mondolfo in Rome and Elizabeth Cox in London. Their assistance has been invaluable.

And lastly, we hope the reader will find this book a practical, no-nonsense kind of cookbook. One to be looked at and enjoyed, but, above all, to be used.

Buon Appetito!

How to Please Your Pasta

(and make oodles of beautiful noodles)

A basic guide to some of the Dos and Donts of pasta cooking.

Pasta-making

Store-bought pasta, even the domestically produced kind, is usually of excellent quality. However, like most other commercially produced foods, it is never quite as good as the homemade variety. So I feel everyone should give pasta-making a try. It is not as difficult as it may sound and is a very satisfying thing to do. Of course pasta-making is a necessary task for the preparation of ravioli and tortellini; these are of doubtful quality when store-bought.

Making the dough is really easy; rolling it out requires a little practice. If you are doing it for the first time, don't make it on a busy day. Slowly does it. And remember to keep your working surface well floured at all times; pasta dough gets quite sticky when it is rolled out. Don't worry about too much flour sticking to the dough – it will all come off in the cooking water.

To make egg-noodle dough
4 large eggs
4 tablespoons cold water
about 1 pound (4 cups) all-purpose flour
1 Break the eggs into a large mixing bowl. Add the water and about a quarter of the flour. Beat this mixture with a wire whisk until it is very smooth.
2 Add nearly all the rest of the flour and work the mixture with your hands into a soft dough. If the dough seems sticky, work in the rest of the flour. (The absorbency of the flour can vary from one bag to the next, as can the size of the eggs.)
3 Turn the dough out onto a kneading surface and knead it well for 10 minutes, just as you would a bread dough. This will extract the gluten content in the flour and give the dough its elasticity.

4 Put the dough back in the bowl, cover it and leave it to rest for at least 20 minutes. (In no way can the dough be rolled out until *after* a lengthy rest period; it would just pull back on you.)
5 Roll the dough out to a thickness of $\frac{1}{8}$ inch. You may find it easier to cut the dough into two pieces first, and roll them out separately. They will be more manageable that way.

To make green-noodle dough
One 10-oz package frozen chopped spinach, cooked, or 1 pound fresh spinach, cooked and chopped finely
4 large eggs
$\frac{3}{4}$–1 pound (3–4 cups) all-purpose flour
1 Drain the cooked spinach well and squeeze as much as possible to remove the cooking water. The more expert you are at this, the less flour you will need, and your noodles will be greener.
2 Break the eggs into a mixing bowl. Add the spinach and a quarter of the flour. Beat well with a wire whisk until the mixture is smooth.
3 Add the rest of the flour gradually, then follow the instructions for egg-noodle dough from stage 2 down.

Pasta by Machine

For those cooks who become pasta addicts, it is well worth acquiring a pasta machine. The machines make an excellent job of kneading and rolling out the pasta and cutting the noodles. And it needn't be an expensive machine, either. The cheaper ones are just as efficient at rolling out the dough, but they have fewer blades and don't cut quite as many different shapes. But they all cut egg noodles and flat sheets, really the basic requirements.

Shaping of Pasta

Shaping the pasta is the fun part. There are hundreds of different pasta shapes. The basic commercial ones are passed through dies and emerge as long, solid rods. These are spaghetti of various thicknesses. The next step is to push a metal rod through the solid strand, and these emerge as macaroni. Then come all the fancy shapes of twists, curls, shells, rings, ribbons, tubes, stars, etc. The easiest and most popular ones to make at home are those cut from flat sheets of pasta, which are then called noodles. You make these as follows:

Roll the flat sheet of dough up from one side to the other, like a jelly-roll (Swiss roll), and cut slices off it with a sharp knife. Unroll the slices and lay the noodles flat on a piece of well-floured waxed or grease-proof paper. Leave them to dry for 10–15 minutes before cooking.

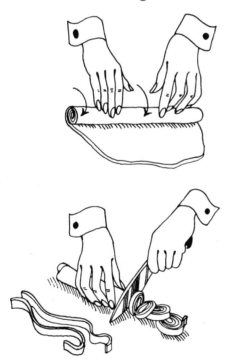

For tagliatelle: cut the roll into ½-inch thick slices
For fettuccine: cut the roll into ¼-inch thick slices
For fettucce: cut the roll into ½–¾-inch thick slices

Pappardelle are cut from a flat sheet of dough into strips about ⅝ inch wide. Cut them with a fluted pastry wheel rather than a knife; this will give the noodles their characteristic edges. Dry them for only 5 minutes before cooking.

Also from flat sheets are cut the following:
manicotti: cut into 3-inch squares
lasagne: cut into 4 × 10-inch rectangles
cannelloni: cut into 4-inch squares
(Don't dry any of these; cook them as soon as you can.)

Any left over pasta dough can be gathered into a ball and rolled out again, to be cut into noodles, or it can be cut into small squares for soups. These are called pastina or quadrucci.

Storing Pasta

Noodles which are not cooked straight away after the specified drying period should be left out on floured waxed paper until they are completely dry. This takes at least one day. They will then resemble commercially produced pasta and should be stored as such, in paper bags or cardboard boxes, to allow for air circulation. Dried pasta will keep for months without refrigeration.

Filled pasta such as ravioli and tortellini cannot be dried because the filling will spoil. They can, however, be frozen. Place them in rows on floured waxed paper, not touching or they will stick together. Roll them up in the waxed paper, then wrap the roll in foil and freeze.

Cooking of Pasta

Pasta needs to be cooked in a large pot, with plenty of water to float around in. It should never be crowded into a pot or it will stick together. For the same reason you should not use a metal spoon for stirring; a wooden spoon or, better still, a wooden fork does a much more efficient job.

As a rule, 1 pound of pasta requires at least 4 quarts of water and 1–1½ tablespoons of salt. But do not add the salt until the water boils, and only just before the pasta goes in, otherwise you get an odd side taste. The pot should never be more than partially covered.

Long, thin pasta should not be broken into pieces. Immerse it as far as it will go in boiling water; let it fan out at the top. Then bend in the middle and force the rest under water with a wooden fork. Other pastas should all go into the pot at the same time, otherwise some of it will be cooked more quickly than the rest, and nothing is as bad as overboiled pasta.

Store-bought pasta cooks much longer than fresh, homemade pasta. Follow the package directions, or better still, bite a piece now and then. The pasta should be soft, but with a slight resilience in the centre. This is the *al dente* stage, and the stage at which most Italians serve their pasta. However, you may like yours a little bit harder or softer than that, but bear in mind, it should never be mushy.

Homemade, fresh pasta cooks very fast:

Egg noodles, yellow	5–6 minutes approximately
Egg noodles, green	4–5 minutes approximately
Lasagne	2 minutes
Manicotti	2 minutes
Cannelloni	2 minutes
Tortellini	5–8 minutes
Ravioli	5–8 minutes

These are rough guides; the best guides are your teeth. As a general rule, home-made pasta is cooked when it rises to the top of the pot.

Pasta Serving

Most commonly pasta used to be served as a first or second course, to be followed by the main course or entrée. It is still frequently served this way in many restaurants in Italy, but at home it has become more of a main dish. This seems to be the way most people prefer their pasta.

If pasta is served as a first course, 2–3 ounces of pasta per person is plenty. It should then be served in rimmed, small bowls and eaten with a fork.

However, if pasta is served as a main course, you have to judge the amount of pasta per person by your guests' appetites. Main-meal pasta can be served on a dinner plate, and it makes a delicious, satisfying and usually inexpensive meal when served with some fresh crusty bread and a crisp tossed salad. Followed by some fresh fruit, this is one of the most nutritious meals you can serve.

Cheeses for Pasta

The most commonly used cheeses in pasta cookery are cheeses for grating. And the two most popular and easily obtainable ones are parmesan and romano, in that order. Ideally it is best to use the imported kinds, for their quality is immensely superior to the domestic variety. However, if you cannot get the imported kinds, domestic brands are adequate. Real imported parmesan should be at least three years old and golden in color. Romano cheese is white.

Neither cheese should ever be bought already grated. Once grated they soon lose their pungency and taste of very little more than plastic. No complement to a lovingly prepared dish. Do not grate the cheeses until just before you plan to use them.

Grated parmesan is passed with just about every dish of pasta, but never with fishy ones. The sharp flavor would distract too much from the delicate taste of the fish.

Ricotta cheese is used mainly for fillings of stuffed pasta and is readily available in most large supermarkets. Cottage cheese, which looks similar, is only a substitute, which should only be used if ricotta is absolutely unavailable.

Mozzarella cheese is commonly used in baked dishes, since it acquires its characteristic stringyness only when it is hot. It is a mild, somewhat creamy, cheese.

Ingredients in Pasta Cooking

Most of the different kinds of pasta used in this book are easily obtainable. Supermarkets carry a surprising variety. Grocery stores in Italian neighbourhoods are a fine source, of course. If you have trouble tracking down a particular shape, ask your grocer to get it. It is not difficult for him to find it among the many brands on the market.

The herbs in this book are also readily available in dried form. Fresh ones one never sees in the supermarkets, but they are such fun to grow in the garden or in a flowerpot.

Most people believe that the Italians use a lot more garlic than they do. Indeed, many use it only sparingly. Then there are people who consider garlic in a sautéed form too heavy to digest, and prefer to add it later, together with the sauce. See which way you like best. There is also a rule that if a dish contains tomatoes, any cooking oil may be used for the sauté stage. However, if a dish does not contain tomatoes, olive oil is essential to enhance the authentic flavors.

Any pasta used in this book may be exchanged for another shape of pasta if desired. There are no hard and fast rules as to what goes with what. Personally, I do prefer the larger pasta shapes with those succulent meat sauces, so the sauce will cling to the grooves, little bits of meat get stuck in the crevices and fill up the inside – yum!

The meat content in my recipes is usually rather higher than Italian cookbooks suggest. This is because I believe that most people will want to serve pasta as a main course. As indeed a lot of Italians do. So the nutritious value of the dishes has been taken into account. Four ounces of meat per person does not seem extravagant. Italian cookbooks usually suggest 2 ounces per person. I prefer to give up authenticity for nutritious value here.

Of course, the pasta itself, even the store-bought variety, has a high nutritious value, being made of good flour or semolina flour with wholesome additions of spinach or eggs, or both.

Note I like to pour off the accumulated fat by setting the lid askew, only leaving a tiny crack for the fat to escape through. You can pour the hot fat straight down the sink, provided the cold tap is running. The cold water will flush the globules down smoothly.

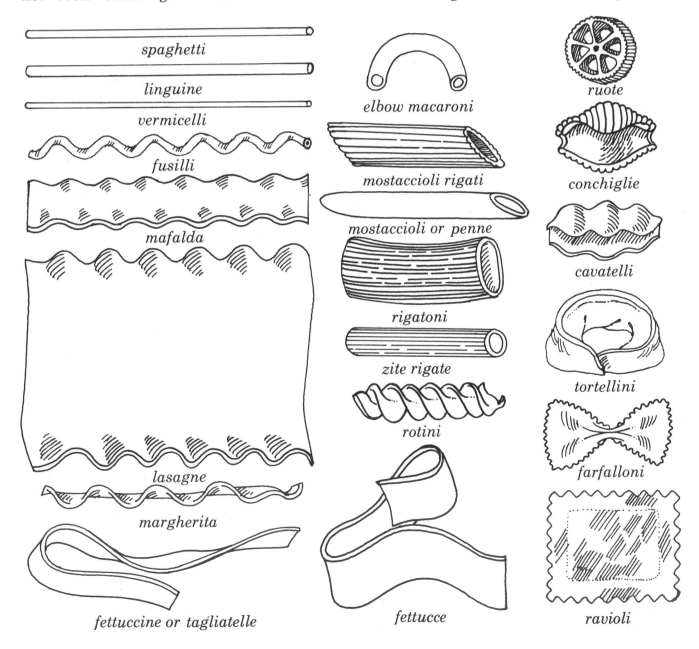

spaghetti

linguine

vermicelli

fusilli

mafalda

lasagne

margherita

fettuccine or tagliatelle

elbow macaroni

mostaccioli rigati

mostaccioli or penne

rigatoni

zite rigate

rotini

fettucce

ruote

conchiglie

cavatelli

tortellini

farfalloni

ravioli

3 tablespoons butter
4 slices bacon, chopped
1 large onion, finely chopped
1 medium carrot, finely chopped
1 stalk celery, finely chopped
2 tablespoons oil
⅓ pound ground beef
⅓ pound ground pork
⅓ pound ground veal

½ cup white wine
2 cups good beef stock
3 tablespoons tomato paste
1 teaspoon dried oregano
a little grated nutmeg
salt and pepper to taste
1 cup heavy cream (or to taste)
1 pound spaghetti
grated parmesan cheese

1 Melt the butter in a frying pan and in it sauté the chopped bacon, onion, carrot and celery. Cook, uncovered, stirring frequently, for about 10 minutes. Set aside till needed.

finely chopped   bacon chopped   finely chopped   finely chopped

2 Heat the oil in a heavy saucepan and in it brown the meats, breaking up any lumps with a wooden spoon, until the mixture is brown and crumbly. Pour off the accumulated fat using the saucepan lid.

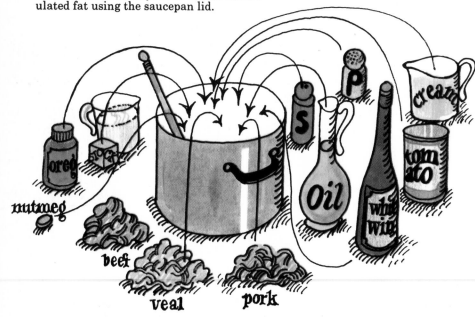

nutmeg   beef   veal   pork

3 Put back on the fire and stir in the wine. Cook over high heat until most of the wine has evaporated. Stir in the beef stock, tomato paste, oregano, nutmeg, salt and pepper, and the reserved vegetables and bacon.

4 Simmer this sauce, only partially covered, until it has reduced to a thick sauce, about 40–60 minutes. Add all or some of the cream, but do not boil again!

5 Cook the spaghetti in plenty of boiling water (add salt when boiling) until *al dente*. Drain.

SPAGHETTI

6 Serve the pasta on hot plates, with some of the sauce spooned on top. Serve plenty of grated parmesan cheese with this dish.

Note This sauce is equally good over any noodle or macaroni, or any of the larger pasta shapes, such as rigatoni or shells.

Spaghetti Bolognese

This was probably your first introduction to pasta as a child – or so you thought. A familiar name – but have you tried the authentic version? The smooth and delicate tasting bolognese sauce is distinguised by the addition of fresh cream and aromatic vegetables. Savor this simple dish and discover the real thing, Bologna style. The children will love it! (Serves 4)

4 tablespoons butter
½ cup heavy cream
6 tablespoons grated parmesan cheese
salt and pepper to taste
8 oz fettucce

1 Melt the butter in a small saucepan over a low heat. Don't let it brown.

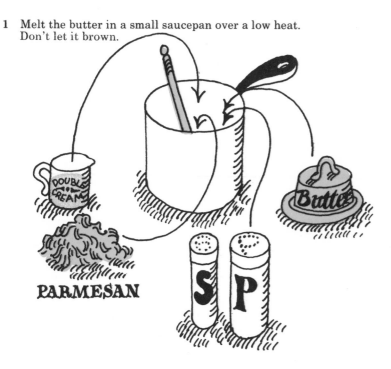

PARMESAN

S P

Butter

DOUBLE CREAM

3 Cook the fettucce in plenty of boiling water (add salt when boiling) until *al dente*. Drain well.

FETTUCCE

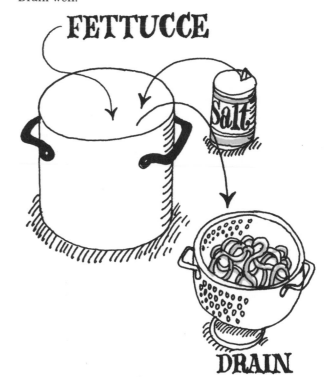

Salt

DRAIN

2 Off the heat add the cream and the grated parmesan. Put back on the fire to heat the sauce through and melt the cheese. Do not boil, however, because of the fresh cream. Stir in the salt and pepper.

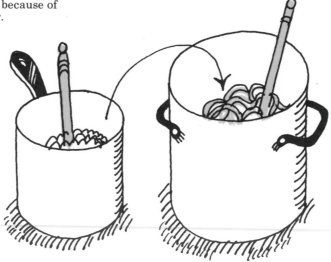

4 Combine the noodles and the sauce and leave to stand, covered, for 2 minutes before serving.

Pass more grated parmesan cheese if you wish.

Note You can substitute fettuccine for fettucce. Homemade noodles are especially fine for this dish.

132

FETTUCCE ALFREDO

This dish is named after Alfredo, owner of the famous
restaurant *Alfredo* in Rome. It makes a first course for four –
one of the pure pasta dishes that distinguish themselves by their earthy
simplicity. It has a delicate, unbelievably creamy taste
and may also be served as a main course or as a
great accompaniment to fried, grilled or roast meats.

1 recipe egg-noodle dough
1 small onion, finely chopped
2 tablespoons oil
1–2 cloves garlic, crushed
1 pound ground beef
2 tablespoons grated parmesan cheese
2 tablespoons chopped parsley
1 teaspoon salt
a little grated nutmeg
one 10-oz package frozen spinach, cooked and chopped
   or 1 pound fresh spinach, cooked and chopped
2 eggs
1 recipe salsa di pomodoro

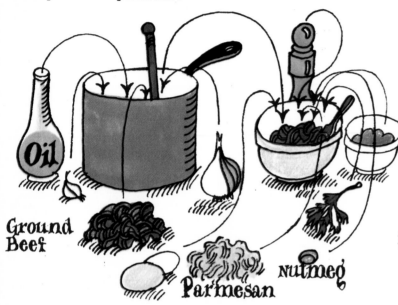

1   To prepare the filling sauté the onion in the oil until soft and transparent. Add the garlic and sauté 1 minute longer. Add the ground beef, turn up the heat slightly, and brown the beef nicely. Break up any lumps with a wooden spoon. When cooked, transfer the mixture to a mixing bowl.

2   To the meat mixture add the cheese, parsley, salt, nutmeg, spinach and eggs. Mix with a fork until well combined.

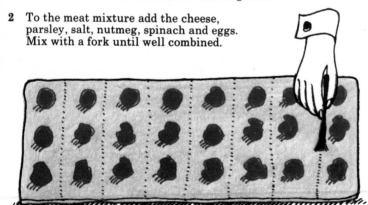

3   Divide the dough into 2 pieces, and roll each one out to a rectangle of ⅛-inch thickness.

4   Place a heaped teaspoon of filling at 2-inch intervals on one of the sheets of dough. With a pastry brush dipped in cold water, dampen a line on the space between the fillings to help seal the ravioli later. Cover the fillings with the other sheet of dough.

5   With your index finger press down between the fillings to seal them in. With a fluted pastry wheel or a sharp

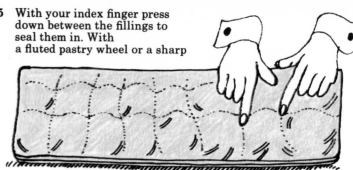

knife, cut the ravioli into 2-inch squares. Seal the edges firmly by pressing the seams together all around, either with your finger or with a fork. Set the ravioli aside on well-floured waxed paper until all ravioli have been made.

6   Cook the ravioli, a few at a time, in plenty of boiling water (add salt when boiling) until *al dente* (8–10 minutes). Drain them by removing them with a slotted spoon and proceed to boil the rest of the ravioli.

Drain

7   Spread a thin layer of the tomato sauce in a baking dish. Lay a single layer of cooked ravioli loosely in the dish. Cover with tomato sauce. Add more ravioli and cover each layer with tomato sauce to keep ravioli from sticking together. Pour leftover sauce over top of dish.

8   To heat the ravioli through, bake the dish, covered with foil, in an oven pre-heated to (325°). This will take 15–30 minutes, depending on how cold they were when going into the oven.

Note   Up to stage 7, ravioli can be made 2–3 hours in advance.

134

A magnificent combination of robust tomato sauce and beef filling gives this dish a full-bodied country flavor. Home-made, old fashioned goodness.

Make them yourself and find out what real home-made Italian ravioli are like. You will surprise and delight family and friends. (Serves 4)

135

This is the quantity per person:

1 tablespoon olive oil
3 slices lean bacon (preferably unsmoked),
  cut into strips
1 egg, beaten
1 heaping teaspoon chopped parsley (optional)
a generous grating of black pepper
3 oz penne
2 tablespoons grated romano _or_ parmesan
  cheese

1   Heat the oil in a saucepan and in it fry the bacon pieces until nicely browned. Remove the bacon with a slotted spoon and leave to drain on paper towels.

4   Boil the penne in plenty of salted water until _al dente_. Do _not_ drain! With a slotted spoon remove the pasta from the water, letting it drain as much as you can. Then drop the steaming hot pasta into the egg mixture. The idea is to keep the pasta so hot that it will set the eggs slightly. Mix it all up well.

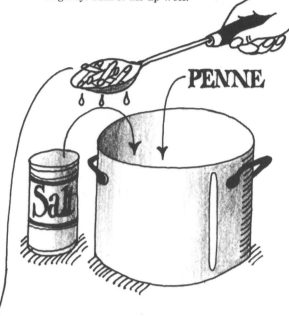

chopped

PENNE

5   Sprinkle on the bacon bits and the romano cheese and toss well.

Serve immediately, with more grated romano if wanted.

2   In a bowl combine the egg, parsley (if used) and pepper with a wire whisk until thoroughly blended.

3   Keep the egg mixture in a warm place until ready to use. (Not too hot though, or the egg would set.)

136

This dish is one of the most popular
in Italy, and it is fast gaining
popularity all over the world. It is one
of the quickest and cheapest of pasta
dishes, so full of goodness that it can be
enjoyed as a main course.
Truly delightful.

PENNE ALLA CARBONARA

½ recipe egg-noodle dough, cut
  into lasagne
  or ½ pound store-bought lasagne
1 recipe ragù bolognese
1 recipe besciamella
5 tablespoons grated parmesan cheese

Bolognese Sauce

Besciamella

1 Cook the lasagne a few at a time in plenty of boiling water
(add salt when boiling) until *al dente*. Drain them
in a colander and leave to cool slightly.

DRAIN

2 Butter generously a large baking dish or casserole
(about 9 × 12 × 3 inches).

3 Spread a thin layer of ragù bolognese over the bottom
of the baking dish. Over it spread ⅓ of the besciamella.
On top of that layer ⅓ of the cooked lasagne, slightly
overlapping. Repeat this process until all the sauces
have been used; finish with a layer of besciamella.
Onto the finished dish sprinkle the parmesan cheese.
(Depending on the size of your dish, there may be
a few noodles left over.)

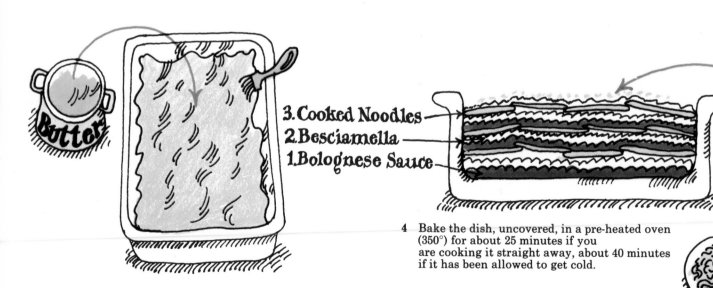

Butter

3. Cooked Noodles
2. Besciamella
1. Bolognese Sauce

4 Bake the dish, uncovered, in a pre-heated oven
(350°) for about 25 minutes if you
are cooking it straight away, about 40 minutes
if it has been allowed to get cold.

Parmesan

Note You can prepare stages 1–3 up to 3 hours in advance.
Cover the dish with foil or plastic wrap until ready to bake.
Instead of besciamella you can use cottage or ricotta cheese
and sliced mozzarella cheese. You will need about 1 pound
of ricotta and 6–8 oz of mozzarella.
Layer (1) bolognese; (2) ricotta; (3) mozzarella; (4) lasagne.
Repeat twice again, finishing with mozzarella.

Lasagne

One of the most substantial of all pasta dishes, extremely popular both in and outside of Italy. A delectable blend of pasta, besciamella and ragù bolognese makes this dish rich and appetizing. Full of nourishment, it takes a little time to prepare but is more than worth the trouble. A delightful winter meal that you will want to come back to even if it's summer. (Serves 4)

2–4 cloves garlic, cut in half
½ teaspoon dried red pepper flakes
2 tablespoons chopped parsley
5 tablespoons olive oil
1 pound thin spaghetti
freshly ground black pepper to taste

2   Cook the spaghetti in plenty of boiling water
(add salt when boiling) until *al dente*. Drain.

1   Sauté the garlic, red pepper flakes and parsley
in the olive oil for 1–2 minutes over a low heat.
Do not let the garlic brown!
Remove the garlic with a slotted spoon and discard.

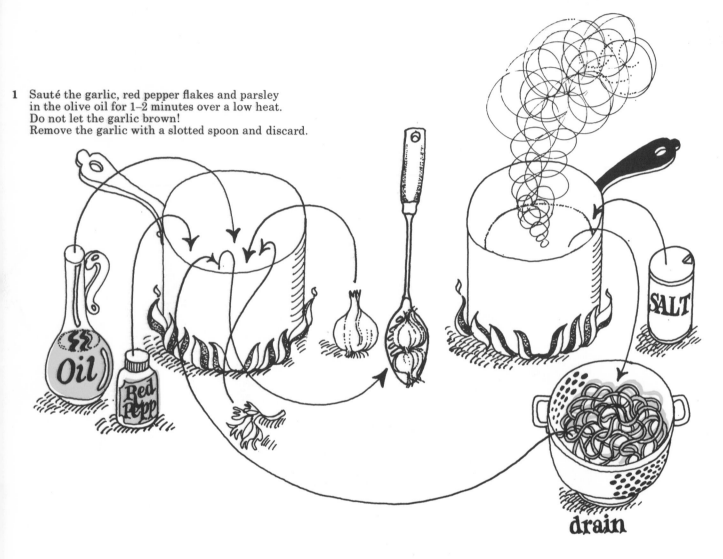

drain

3   Off the heat, mix the hot pasta into the hot oil mixture,
season with black pepper and mix well.

Serve immediately, absolutely piping hot!

Spaghetti Aglio e Olio

One of the pure and basic pasta dishes of Italy. A simple, ingenious combination of garlic and olive oil gives this dish its smooth quality.

Quick to make, tasty and inexpensive, it is an authentic touch of Italy. Try it with a glass of Chianti. (Serves 6 as a first course)

141

1 medium onion, finely chopped
4 tablespoons butter
½ pound mushrooms,
   sliced and the stems chopped
salt and pepper to taste
½ pound unsmoked thinly sliced ham
   or prosciutto, cut into squares
1 cup heavy cream
2 tablespoons chopped parsley
6 oz green noodles
6 oz yellow noodles
6 tablespoons grated parmesan cheese

1 Sauté the onion in the butter
   until soft and transparent.

BUTTER

chopped

S P

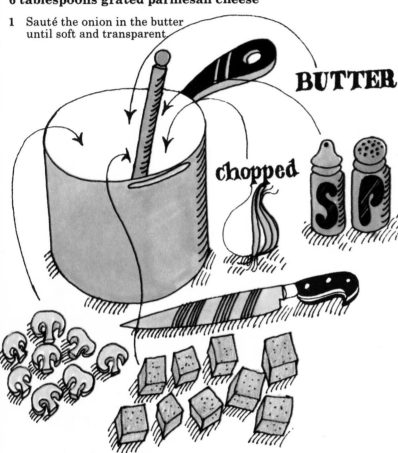

2 Then add the sliced mushrooms and chopped stems,
   turn up the heat slightly, and sauté them until done,
   about 5 minutes. Stir frequently.

3 Add the salt and pepper and the ham squares, and cook
   all together another minute, just to heat through.

4 Add the cream and let everything heat through again, without
   letting the sauce boil. (Be especially careful with fresh
   cream; it may curdle.)
   Then stir in the parsley.

cream

5 Cook the green and yellow noodles separately in plenty of
   boiling water (add salt when boiling) until *al dente*.
   Drain well. (Green noodles cook faster than yellow.)

EGG NOODLES
GREEN NOODLES

Salt

Parmesan

6 Combine the sauce with the noodles, add the parmesan and
   stir well. Leave them, covered, for 2 minutes before serving.
   You can serve more grated parmesan cheese at the table
   if you wish.

Note You can use all yellow noodles for this dish
   if green noodles are not available.

142

Paglia e Fieno

A beautifully creamy dish, full of different tastes,
textures and colors. An extremely ingenious blend that is as appealing to the eye
as it is to the tongue, makes a great main course that's easy to make and never fails to please. (Serves 4)

5 tablespoons butter
2 tablespoons flour
1 cup milk
3 oz gouda cheese
3 oz gruyère cheese
3 oz mozzarella cheese
12 oz mostaccioli
4 tablespoons butter
generous grating of black pepper
3 oz grated parmesan cheese

3 Cook the mostaccioli in plenty of boiling water (add salt when boiling) until *al dente*. Drain. Transfer them to a hot dish, flake the remaining 4 tablespoons of butter into the pasta and toss well.

4 Re-heat the cheese sauce if it has cooled too much, and stir to make sure all the cheeses have melted.

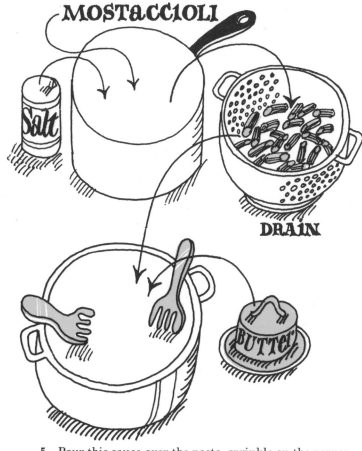

1 To make a white sauce, melt the 5 tablespoons of butter in a saucepan, add the flour all at once, and stir it around until all the flour has been absorbed into the butter. Then add the milk slowly, stirring all the time with a wire whisk, until the sauce starts to thicken. Simmer gently, stirring all the time, for 2 minutes.

5 Pour this sauce over the pasta, sprinkle on the pepper, and toss well to distribute the sauce evenly.

2 Grate the first three cheeses on the coarse side of a grater and stir them into the white sauce. It will melt the cheese.

6 Serve immediately, with the grated parmesan passed separately.

Note Other cheeses you can add or substitute are provolone, fontina, taleggio or emmenthaler. Instead of parmesan you could use asiago. Macaroni or elbow macaroni can be substituted.

Mostaccioli con Quattro Formaggi

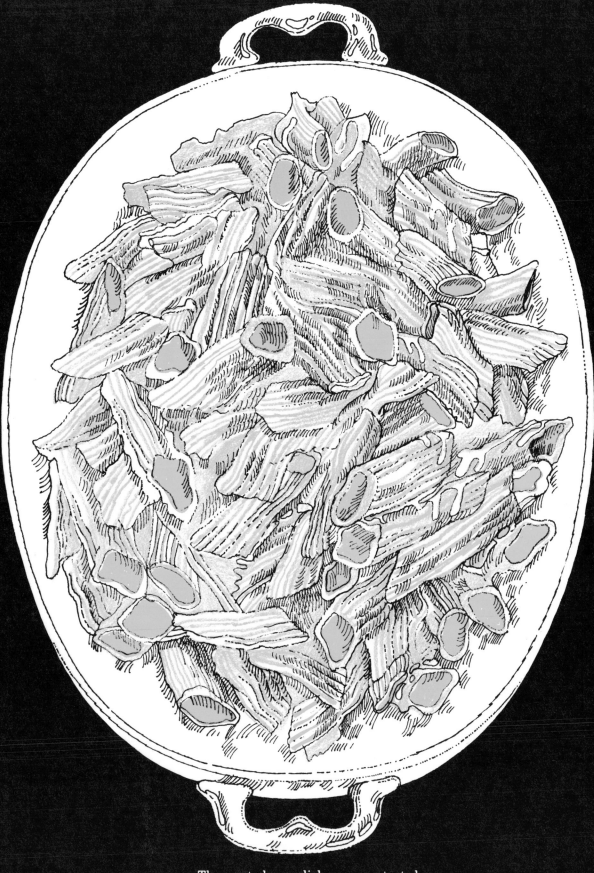

The most cheesy dish you ever tasted.
Full of creamy goodness, with a wonderful bite to it if you use mostaccioli, penne or rigatoni
– the cheese spills over into the holes and you get twice the cheese with every bite. (Serves 4)

18–24 cherrystone clams
7 tablespoons olive oil
3 cloves garlic, cut into quarters
3 tablespoons chopped parsley
¼ teaspoon dried red pepper flakes
¼ teaspoon dried basil
2 shallots *or* 1 small onion, finely chopped
1 cup white wine
1 pound linguine

1   Scrub the clams well with a stiff brush, until all traces of sand have disappeared. You may want to soak them in cold water for a while. Rinse well.

2   Heat the oil in a large saucepan wide enough to accommodate the clams. Put in the garlic quarters and heat them through without browning, just for a minute or two. Remove the garlic with a slotted spoon.

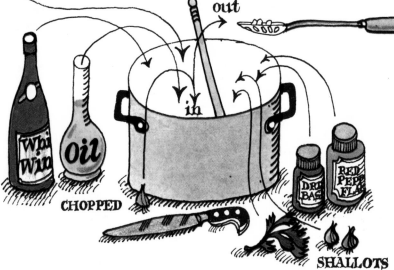

CHOPPED

SHALLOTS

3   To the oil add the parsley, red pepper flakes, basil and shallots or onions and sauté over medium heat, stirring frequently, for about 3 minutes.

4   Add the wine and all the clams, cover and leave to simmer for 7 minutes. After 7 minutes, tilt the pot back and forth a few times to release the clam juices into the wine. Uncover.

5   Remove the clams with a slotted spoon onto a plate and leave to cool slightly. Remove the clams from their shells and cut them into quarters. Put them back into the sauce.

CLAMS NOW OPEN

TAKE OUT   & CHOP

6   Cook the linguine in plenty of boiling water (add salt when boiling) until *al dente*. Drain well.

LINGUINE

7   Transfer the linguine onto a platter and spoon the clam sauce on top.

Serve immediately.

Note   If using canned minced clams follow stages 2 and 3, but at stage 4 use only half the wine and ½ cup of bottled clam juice. Then add the clams and all their juice and cook, uncovered, for 8–10 minutes to reduce the liquid somewhat. Proceed with stages 6 and 7. Instead of linguine, you can use spaghetti.

146

LINGUINE CON VONGOLE

A slightly extravagant seafood dish. The clam juice,
combined with the wine and herbs, produces a beautiful taste and aroma.
A perfect example of the versatility of pasta cookery.
Makes an outstanding first course for six, or a lavish main course for four.

one 2–3 pound chicken
about 5 cups of cold water
1 teaspoon salt
2 tablespoons (1 oz) butter
½ pound fresh mushrooms, sliced
4 tablespoons butter
7 tablespoons flour
2 cups reserved chicken stock
1 cup milk
1 cup heavy cream
salt and pepper to taste
8–12 oz vermicelli
4 tablespoons dry breadcrumbs
4 tablespoons grated parmesan
  cheese

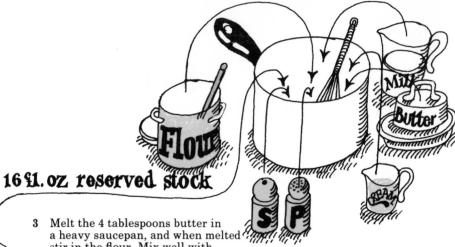

16 fl. oz reserved stock

3   Melt the 4 tablespoons butter in
a heavy saucepan, and when melted
stir in the flour. Mix well with
a wooden spoon or wire whisk, and stir in the reserved stock and the milk.

Cook this mixture over a medium heat until it thickens,
then leave to simmer, stirring all the time, for 3 minutes.
Remove from heat and stir in the cream, salt and pepper.
Add the reserved chicken pieces and the reserved
mushrooms.

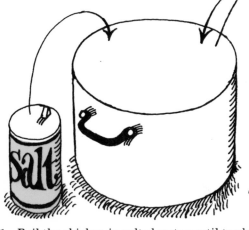

VERMICELLI

1   Boil the chicken in salted water until tender, about
40–50 minutes. Remove the chicken, place on a plate
and leave to cool slightly. Reserve 2 cups
of the cooking water to use as stock. When the chicken
is cool enough to handle, skin and bone it carefully
and cut the meat into bite-size pieces.

2   Melt the 2 tablespoons of butter in a frying pan and
sauté the mushrooms until cooked, stirring frequently.
Reserve.

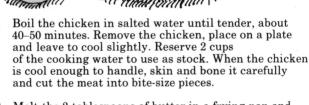

4   Cook the vermicelli in plenty of boiling water
(add salt when boiling) until *al dente*. Drain.

5   Butter a large casserole or ovenproof baking dish. Combine the
sauce and the pasta thoroughly and pour the mixture
into the dish. Smooth the top with the back of a spoon.

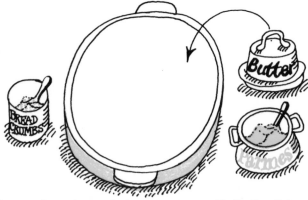

6   Sprinkle the crumbs and grated cheese on top, and bake the dish, uncovered, in a pre-heated (375°) oven for 20–30
minutes. Serve more grated cheese separately if wanted.

Note   This dish can be made up to 2 hours in advance up to stage 5. Keep
covered with foil or plastic until ready to bake. Thin spaghetti
or regular spaghetti can be substituted for vermicelli.

Vermicelli e Pollo

A magnificently smooth, creamy dish. Very attractive and mouthwatering, so subtle it almost melts on the tongue, it makes a luxurious lunch or dinner for a reasonable price. Great as a main course with a tossed salad and a glass of white wine. Bravo! (Serves 4)

1 recipe egg-noodle dough, cut into cannelloni
   or 1 package of 12 store-bought cannelloni
1 medium onion, chopped
2 tablespoons oil
1 clove garlic, chopped
1 pound ground beef
one 10-oz package frozen spinach (*or* 1 lb fresh spinach),
   cooked and chopped
2 beaten eggs
5 tablespoons grated parmesan cheese
3 tablespoons cream *or* evaporated milk
salt, pepper and oregano to taste
more parmesan to taste
1 recipe besciamella sauce
1 recipe tomato sauce

5 In a mixing bowl combine the beef mixture, spinach, eggs, grated parmesan, cream, salt, pepper and oregano. Mix it all up with a fork until well blended.

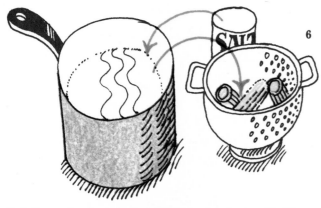

1 Boil the pasta pieces, a few at a time, in plenty of boiling water (add salt when boiling) until *al dente*. Drain and leave to cool slightly.

6 If using homemade squares of dough: place one heaping teaspoon of this filling onto each square of pasta. Fold both sides towards the middle and place each cannelloni, seam side down, into a baking dish which has a thin layer of tomato sauce in it. Don't crowd them, or they will stick together. Store-bought cannelloni tubes can be filled with a teaspoon. Place cannelloni in a single layer all over baking dish. (Scatter leftover filling over them.)

store-bought

homemade

Besciamella

chopped onion

chopped garlic

ground beef

2 Sauté the chopped onion in the oil until soft and transparent. Add the garlic and sauté one minute longer.

3 Add the beef, breaking up any lumps with a wooden spoon, until it is brown and crumbly.

4 Cook the spinach, drain well and leave to cool a little.

7 Distribute the besciamella evenly over the cannelloni. Then cover the besciamella layer with the rest of the tomato sauce, and sprinkle with parmesan.

8 Bake in a pre-heated oven (375°) for 20 minutes if you are baking the dish straight away. If it has been allowed to get cold, bake it for 40 minutes.

Note

This dish can be made up to stage 7 two to three hours in advance. Keep covered with foil or plastic until ready to bake.

Parmesan

150

Cannelloni

Buon Appetito

A truly delectable dish, very popular the world over. The fine combination of meat, spinach and parmesan makes this dish extremely rich in protein. It is very filling and makes a great main course if served with crusty warm bread, a tossed salad and a glass of red wine. Who could ask for anything more? (Serves 4–6)

3 tablespoons butter
1 can tuna fish in oil (6–7 oz)
2 tablespoons finely chopped parsley
1 cup heavy cream
salt and pepper to taste
8 oz margherita

3   Cook the margherita in plenty of boiling water
    (add salt when boiling) until *al dente*.
    Drain thoroughly.

MARGHERITA

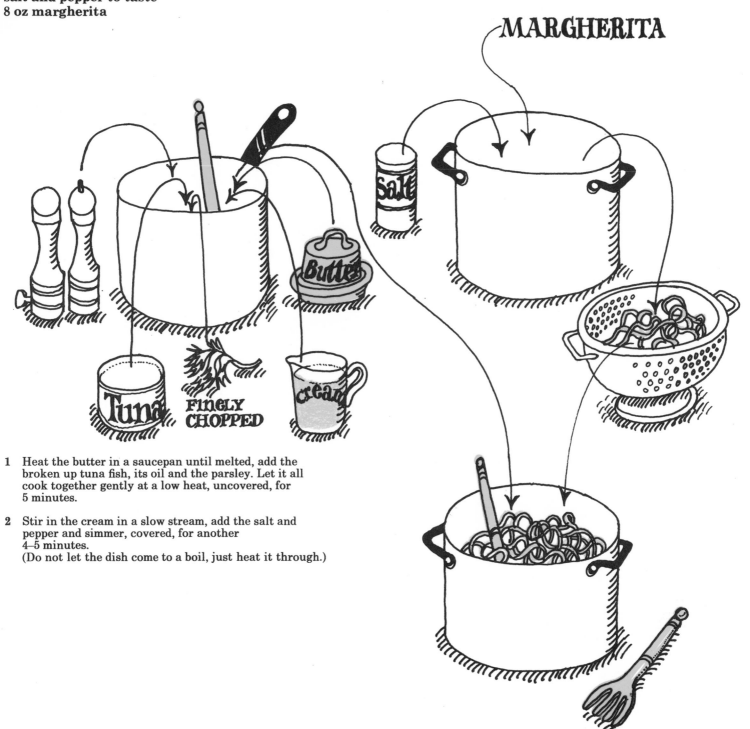

1   Heat the butter in a saucepan until melted, add the
    broken up tuna fish, its oil and the parsley. Let it all
    cook together gently at a low heat, uncovered, for
    5 minutes.

2   Stir in the cream in a slow stream, add the salt and
    pepper and simmer, covered, for another
    4–5 minutes.
    (Do not let the dish come to a boil, just heat it through.)

4   Mix the margherita with the tuna sauce, preferably using
    two wooden forks, until well blended.

Serve immediately.

Note   Tagliatelle or fettuccine can be substituted for margherita.

MARGHERITA CON TONNO

A piquant pasta dish, that is at the same time creamy and delicate. Very easy to prepare, fairly inexpensive to make, and a good way to please your friends when you are in a hurry.

And, it's just what children like – tuna fish and noodles. This dish serves two as a delightful lunch, or four as a first course.

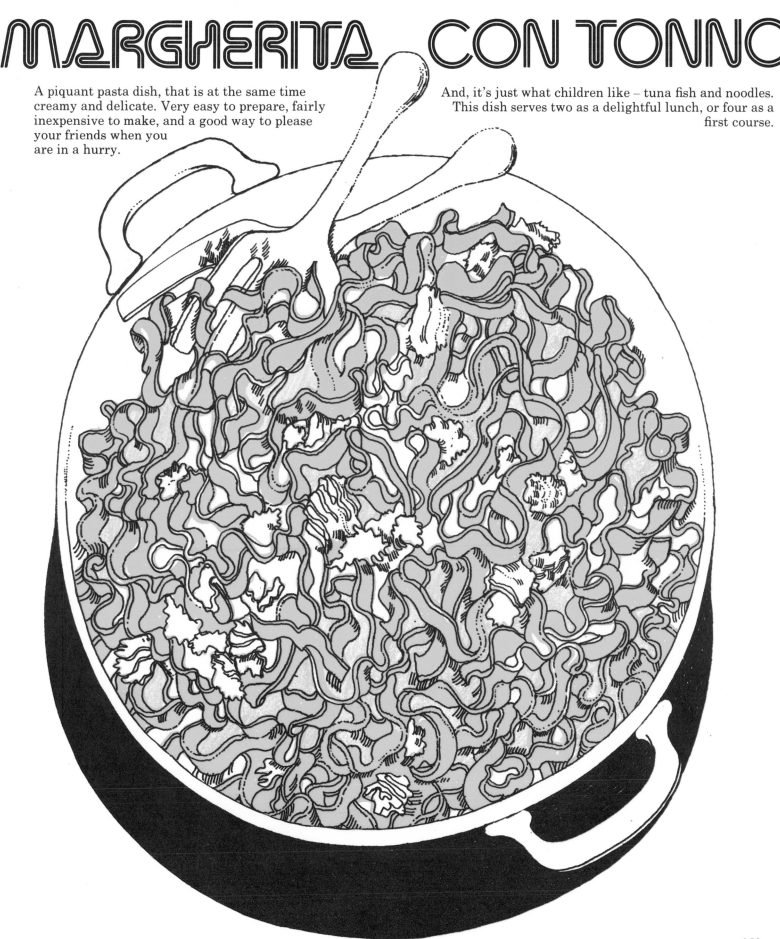

1 onion, finely chopped
3 tablespoons oil
2 cloves garlic, crushed
3 pounds fresh tomatoes,
  skinned and chopped
salt and pepper to taste
1 teaspoon sugar
½ teaspoon dried basil
1 pound raw shrimp, peeled
1 cup white wine
2 tablespoons chopped parsley
1 pound linguine

1 Sauté the onion in the oil until soft
   and transparent. Add the garlic and
   sauté one minute longer.

3 Meanwhile, in another saucepan, simmer the peeled shrimp in
   the wine for 3–4 minutes. Add them to the tomatoes when the
   tomatoes are cooked. Also
   add the chopped parsley and
   let it all simmer another
   4–5 minutes.

4 Boil the linguine in plenty of boiling water (add
   salt when boiling) until *al dente*. Drain.

5 Mix the linguine and the shrimp sauce until well combined. Divide the pasta between six small individual
   dishes, and spoon any sauce that has accumulated in
   the bottom of the saucepan over the pasta.

   Serve immediately.

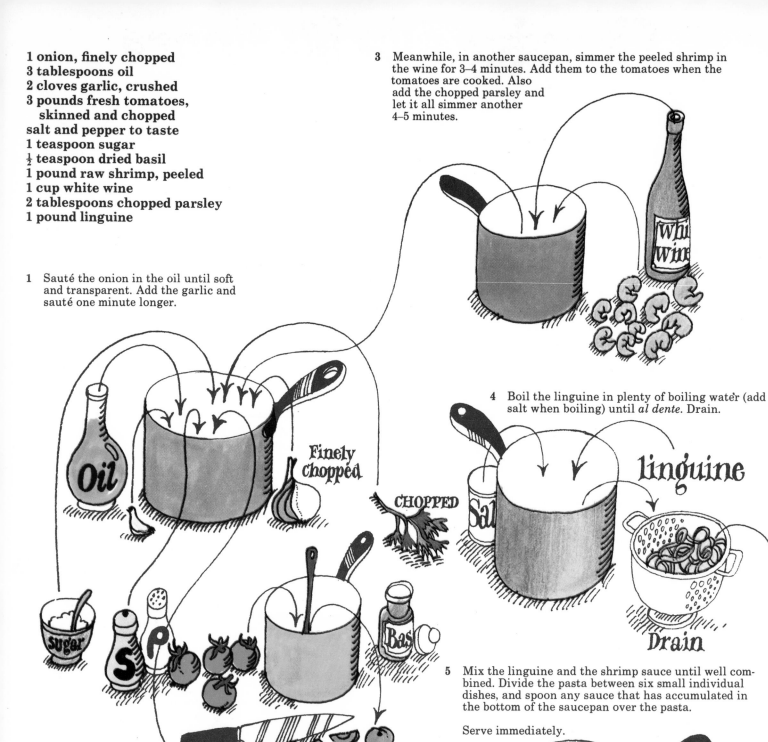

2 Put the tomatoes in the saucepan with the onions, together with
   the salt, pepper, sugar and basil. Simmer slowly, uncovered,
   for 20 minutes.

Note Use only raw shrimp for this dish.
Spaghetti can be substituted for linguine.

Linguine alla Marinara

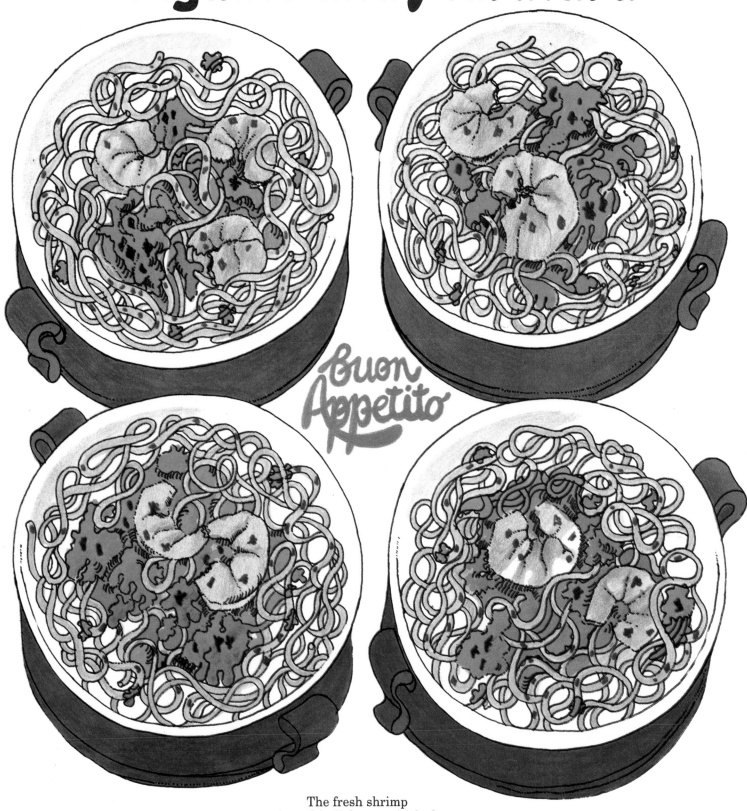

Buon Appetito

The fresh shrimp
gives this dish a particularly
distinguished flavor typical of the Adriatic
coast. The fresh tomatoes add color and gusto. It is the combination
of these light authentic flavors that makes this dish especially pleasant
as a first course in summer. (Serves 6)

1 recipe green-noodle dough
cut into tagliatelle
or **12 oz** green noodles, store-bought
¼–⅜ **pound soft butter**
1–3 cloves garlic, crushed
8 tablespoons grated parmesan cheese
black pepper and salt to taste

1   Cook the tagliatelle in plenty of water (add salt
    when boiling) until *al dente*. Drain.

3   Mix the noodles with the hot garlic butter,
    toss quickly, then add the parmesan cheese and
    pepper and salt. Toss again.

    Serve immediately.

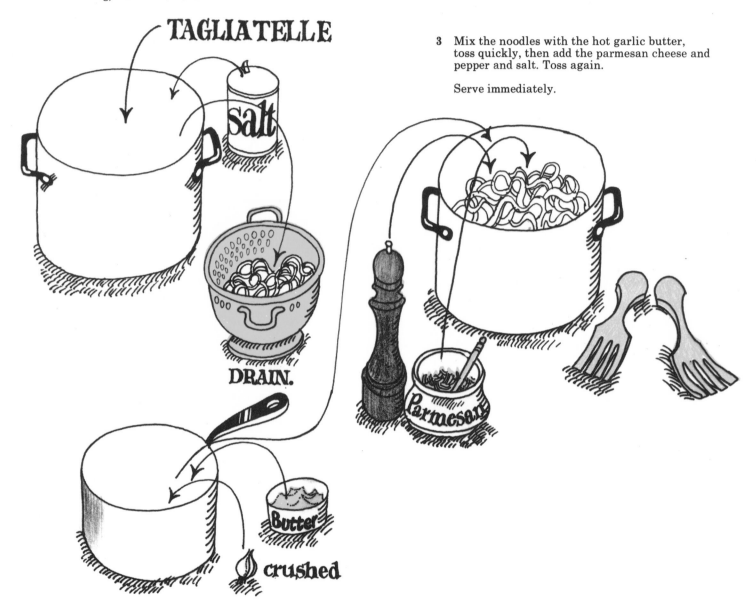

TAGLIATELLE

salt

DRAIN.

Parmesan

Butter

crushed

2   While the pasta is cooking, heat the butter in another
    saucepan and sauté the garlic in it over a very low heat.
    Do not let either the butter or the garlic brown.
    Sauté only for a minute.

Note   This recipe is especially good
           with homemade green noodles.

156

TAGLIATELLE VERDI CON AGLIO

One of those melt-in-the-mouth pasta dishes, incredibly smooth and creamy, with a glorious color and a mild or strong garlic flavor, whichever you prefer. A marvelous first course for four or five, or a great side dish with fried, roast or grilled meat.

1½ pounds ricotta cheese
2 beaten eggs
3 tablespoons finely chopped parsley
a little grated nutmeg
2 tablespoons grated parmesan *or* **romano cheese**
2 oz grated *or* **finely chopped mozzarella cheese**
1 recipe egg-noodle dough
   cut into manicotti,
   or **1 package of 12 store-bought manicotti**
double the recipe for tomato sauce
5 tablespoons grated parmesan

1   Drain the ricotta cheese well.

2   Place the ricotta in a mixing bowl, add the eggs, parsley, nutmeg and the grated cheeses. Blend well with a fork.

parsley~
finely chopped

eggs~beaten

158

3   Cook the manicotti in plenty of boiling water (add salt when boiling) until *al dente*. (Cook a few at a time.) Drain and leave to cool slightly.

drain

4   If using homemade pasta squares, place a heaping tablespoon of cheese filling on each rectangle, then fold both sides towards the middle to cover the filling. (Store-bought manicotti tubes can be filled with a teaspoon.)

store~bought

homemade
square

5   Spread a thin layer of the tomato sauce in a buttered, ovenproof baking dish. Lay the manicotti, seam side down and not touching, in a single layer in the dish. Pour the rest of the tomato sauce over the top.

6   Sprinkle the parmesan cheese on top and bake, uncovered, in a pre-heated (325°) oven for about 30 minutes.

Note   This dish can be made up to 2 hours in advance up to stage 5. Keep the dish covered with foil or plastic until ready to put it in the oven.

Manicotti

In outward appearance manicotti somewhat resemble
cannelloni. However, this manicotti recipe oozes its own taste of a
savory cheese filling topped with a delicious tomato sauce.
Extremely satisfying, very Italian and very appetizing. (Serves 4–6)

2 tablespoons oil
1 large onion, finely chopped
1–2 cloves garlic, crushed (optional)
1 green pepper, cut into strips
black pepper to taste
dried tarragon to taste
1 recipe tomato sauce
1 pound cod *or* sole *or* haddock, cubed
1 pound tagliatelle

1   Heat the oil in a heavy saucepan, then add the chopped onion, crushed garlic, green pepper strips and sauté it all until soft, about 8 minutes. Then add the black pepper and tarragon.

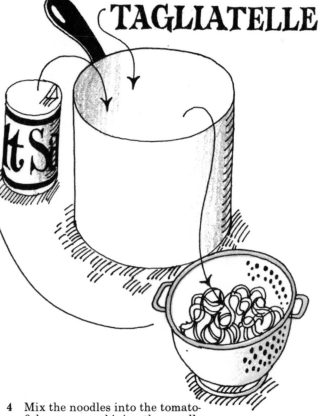

tomato sauce

FISH

TAGLIATELLE

3   Cook the tagliatelle in plenty of boiling water (add salt when boiling) until *al dente*. Drain.

4   Mix the noodles into the tomato-fish sauce, combining them well.

2   To the saucepan add the tomato sauce and the chunks of fish. Cook the dish, uncovered, for about 10 minutes, until the fish is tender but not falling apart.

Tagliatelle e Pesce

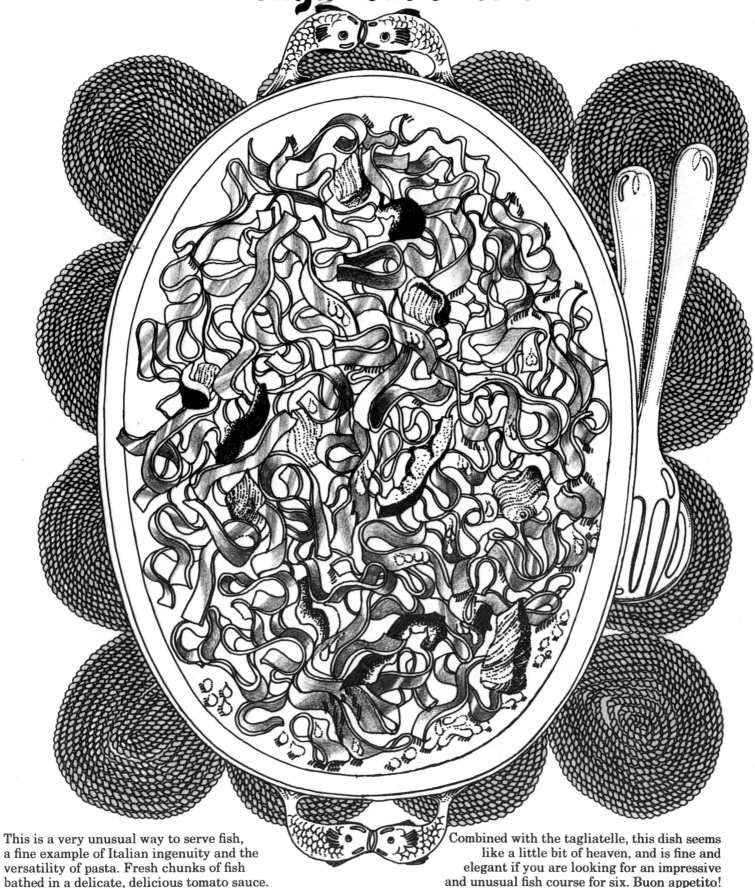

This is a very unusual way to serve fish, a fine example of Italian ingenuity and the versatility of pasta. Fresh chunks of fish bathed in a delicate, delicious tomato sauce.

Combined with the tagliatelle, this dish seems like a little bit of heaven, and is fine and elegant if you are looking for an impressive and unusual fish course for six. Buon appetito!

3 tablespoons butter
1 pound fresh mushrooms,
 whole if small, sliced if large
2 tablespoons oil
1 pound ground pork
1–2 cloves garlic, crushed
½ teaspoon dried basil
½ teaspoon dried oregano

salt and pepper to taste
½ cup white wine
2 tablespoons flour
3 tablespoons tomato paste
1 cup beef stock
12 oz farfalloni
freshly grated parmesan
 cheese

4 Add the tomato paste and the stock. Stir well, cover, and leave to simmer over a low flame for about 20 minutes. Stir quite often to prevent it burning. When done, add the reserved mushrooms.

1 In a saucepan melt the butter and over medium heat sauté the mushrooms until cooked, stirring often. Set aside.

FARFALLONI

5 Cook the farfalloni in plenty of boiling water (add salt when boiling) until *al dente*. Drain.

6 Mix together the farfalloni and the meat-mushroom sauce and serve immediately. Pass the grated parmesan separately.

2 In another saucepan heat the oil and brown the pork in it, breaking up any lumps with a wooden spoon. At this point I like to pour off all the fat.
Stir into the meat the garlic, basil, oregano, salt and pepper. Leave to cook for 2 minutes.

Note This sauce can be made hours in advance; just reheat it while the pasta is cooking.
This dish is also good when made with egg noodles of any width.

3 Turn up the heat and pour in the wine. Let it boil rapidly until the foam subsides. Then add in all the flour, stirring well.

Farfalloni con Funghi

A beautifully rich, brown mushroom-
and-pork sauce with a subtle flavoring.
Delicious and really great with a glass of
red wine and a fresh tossed salad, this juicy
recipe has interesting texture and color. Great family fare –
or treble the recipe and have all your friends in. Buon appetito!
(Serves 4)

12 oz fettuccine
½ cup heavy cream
4–8 tablespoons softened butter
8 tablespoons grated parmesan cheese
6 oz fresh or frozen peas, cooked
½ pound thinly sliced prosciutto *or* boiled ham,
** cut into thin strips**
black pepper to taste

3   Drain the fettuccine, pour them back into the pot and quickly toss in the flaked soft butter and the parmesan.

1   Cook the fettuccine in plenty of boiling water (add salt when boiling) until *al dente*.

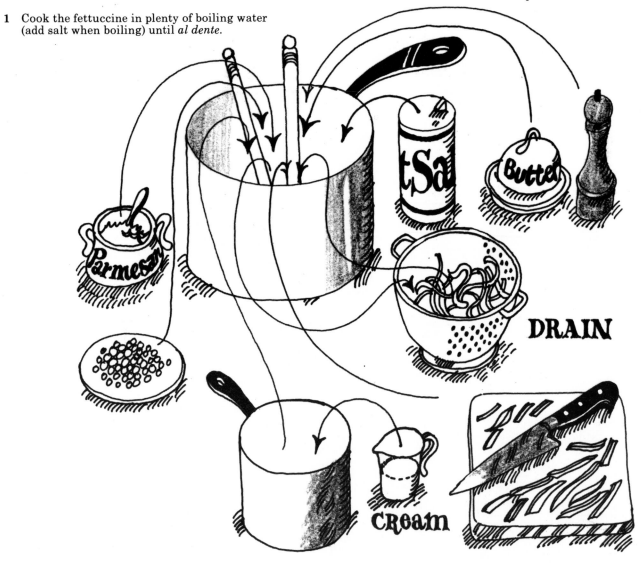

DRAIN

cream

2   While the pasta is cooking, heat the cream in a small saucepan.

4   Add the hot cream, the peas, the prosciutto and black pepper and toss again.

Serve immediately.

Fettuccine alla Romana

A deliciously creamy, colorful dish, the way it is served in Rome.
One of our many favorites, just too good for words, super for a quick lunch.
Invite your friends, bring out the wine and the good conversation.
Buon appetito. (Serves 4)

2 tablespoons oil
1 onion, finely chopped
1 red pepper (green if red is unavailable), cut into strips
1 clove garlic, chopped
1 tablespoon chopped parsley
½ pound lean bacon, cut into strips
1 pound fresh tomatoes, peeled and roughly chopped
   ***or* 1 (16 oz) can tomatoes**
generous grating of black pepper
12 oz spaghetti
2 tablespoons oil
4 tablespoons grated parmesan *or* romano cheese

1 Heat the oil in a saucepan and add the onion, red or green
   pepper, garlic, parsley and bacon. Sauté for about 5 minutes,
   uncovered and stirring often.

2 To this mixture add the tomatoes and pepper. Simmer this dish,
   uncovered, for 15 minutes. Add a little salt then if necessary.

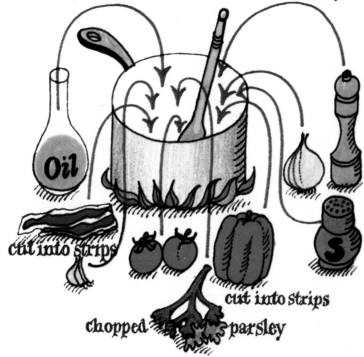

4 Place the spaghetti in a hot bowl,
   sprinkle on the oil and cheese and toss well.

3 Cook the spaghetti in plenty of boiling water
   (add salt when boiling) until *al dente*. Drain.

5 Serve the pasta in individual small bowls,
   with the sauce spooned on top.

   Serve immediately.

Note The sauce itself can be made several hours
   in advance and reheated.

Spaghetti all'Amatriciana

Spaghetti All'Amatriciana takes its name from Amatrice, a small town north of Rome, famous because generations of grocers came from there. Fullbodied and robust taste, a juicy blend of pasta, vegetables, meat and cheese. A great light lunch for three or four, or a first course for five or six.

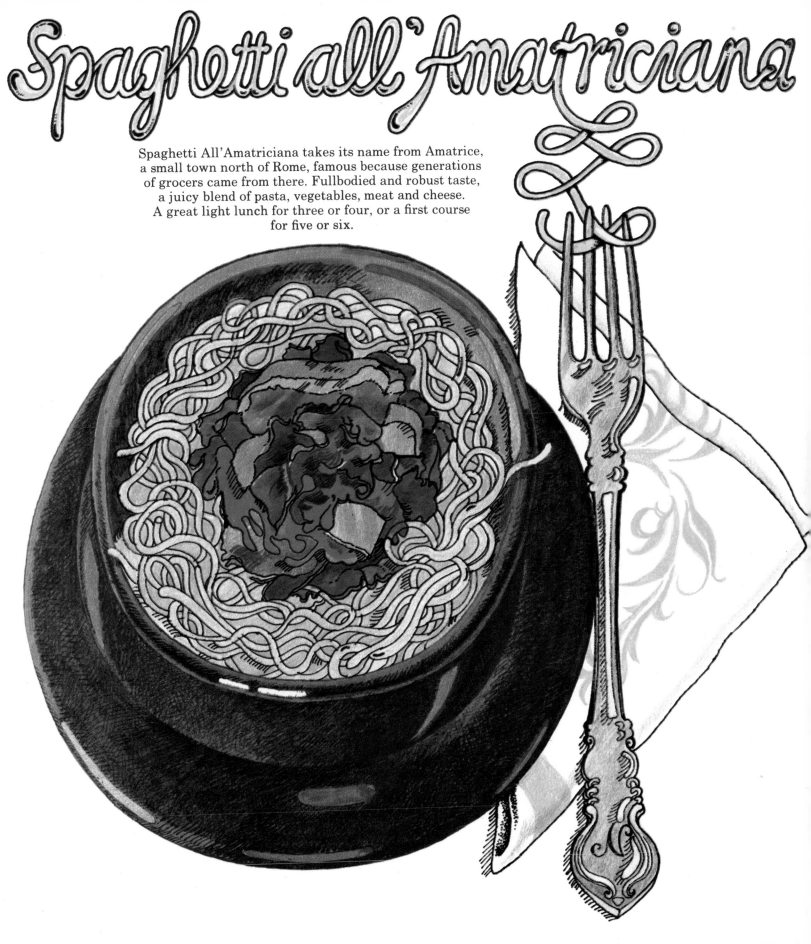

1 medium sized eggplant
salt
6 medium sized tomatoes, peeled,
  seeded and chopped
1–2 cloves garlic, crushed
1–2 tablespoons parsley, chopped
½ teaspoon dried red pepper flakes
2 tablespoons butter
enough oil for frying eggplant
1 pound spaghetti

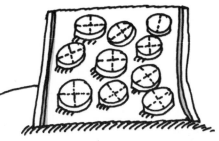

3 In a frying pan sauté the eggplant slices in some hot oil. They will absorb the oil quite quickly, so keep adding more as needed. Fry the slices till they are golden brown on both sides.

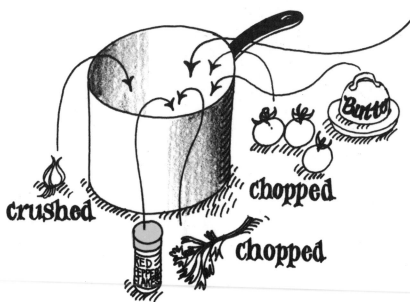

4 Drain the slices on paper towels to absorb the excess fat, then cut them into halves or quarters, and add them to the tomato sauce. Heat through again while the pasta is cooking. Taste for seasoning.

5 Cook the spaghetti in plenty of boiling water (add salt when boiling) until *al dente*. Drain.

1 Cut off both ends of the eggplant and cut the remaining piece into ¼-inch-thick slices. Put the slices into a non-metal bowl, sprinkle a little salt on them, and leave them to drain for 30–45 minutes. After that, dry them thoroughly with paper towels.

SPAGHETTI

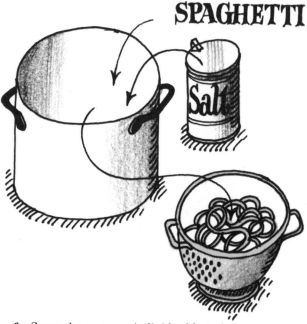

crushed   chopped

chopped

6 Serve the pasta on individual hot plates, with the sauce spooned on top.

2 Meanwhile sauté the chopped tomatoes, garlic, parsley and red pepper flakes in the butter in a saucepan for about 5 minutes. Reserve.

168

A delightful light summer lunch, colorful and unusual.
You can taste the summer goodness of fresh vegetables,
a truly Sicilian combination of tastes.
The more you eat it, the more you'll like it.
(Serves 4)

1 recipe egg-noodle dough
1 pound ricotta cheese
2 oz parmesan cheese, grated
3 tablespoons chopped parsley
a little salt and pepper
1 medium egg

a little grated nutmeg
1 recipe either tomato sauce, bolognese sauce *or*
   beef sauce *or* just melted butter and
   parmesan cheese
grated parmesan cheese

1 Prepare the filling by combining in a bowl the ricotta, parmesan, parsley, salt, pepper, egg and nutmeg. Blend it all well with a fork.

Parmesan **nutmeg**

2 Roll out the dough to $\frac{1}{8}$-inch thickness. Cut the dough into 2-inch circles, with a biscuit-cutter or glass of that diameter.

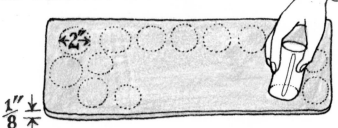

$\frac{1''}{8}$

3 Place about $\frac{1}{2}$ teaspoon of filling on each circle.

4 Fold the top end of the circle over the filling to line up with the bottom end. Press down on the seam all around to seal it well. Then, holding the straight edge against the back of your index finger, pull both the corners towards you to meet in front of your finger. Press the two corners firmly together.

5 Place the finished tortellini in a single layer (not allowing them to touch) on a well-floured waxed paper or greaseproof paper and proceed to shape the rest.

6 Boil the tortellini, a few at a time, in plenty of boiling water (add salt when boiling) until *al dente*. Drain well.

Drain

7 Serve hot, with one of the sauces spooned on top. Serve plenty of grated parmesan cheese separately.

Note You can make tortellini a few hours ahead. Keep them on a well-floured, paper-lined tray, not touching one another, and dust them heavily with flour. Keep refrigerated until ready to use.

Tortellini

One of the glorious stuffed-pasta dishes. When served without a meat-sauce they are called Tortellini da Vigilia (lean tortellini). They are served thus on religious holidays, when the eating of meat is not permitted. (Serves six as a first course, four as a main course.)

1 pound lean lamb, cubed
salt and pepper to taste
¼ teaspoon dried rosemary
3 tablespoons oil
1–2 cloves garlic, chopped
⅜ cup white wine
1 pound fresh tomatoes,
  peeled and chopped
¾–1 cup beef stock
8 oz cavatelli
grated parmesan cheese

1   Season the lamb cubes with a little salt, pepper and rosemary.

2   Heat the oil in a saucepan over fairly high heat and brown the meat cubes on all sides. Add the garlic and cook 1 minute longer.

3   Pour the wine over the meat and let it boil, uncovered, until the foam subsides.

4   Stir in the tomatoes and stock and simmer, only partially covered, for 1–1½ hours. Stir frequently. The sauce will reduce to about half and be fairly thick. Adjust seasoning.

5   Cook the cavatelli in plenty of boiling water (add salt when boiling) until *al dente*. Drain.

6   Combine the pasta and the sauce, then stir in the parmesan cheese.

Serve immediately, with plenty of freshly grated parmesan passed separately.

Note   Instead of cavatelli you can use macaroni, rotini, mostaccioli, rigatoni, conchiglie or farfalloni.

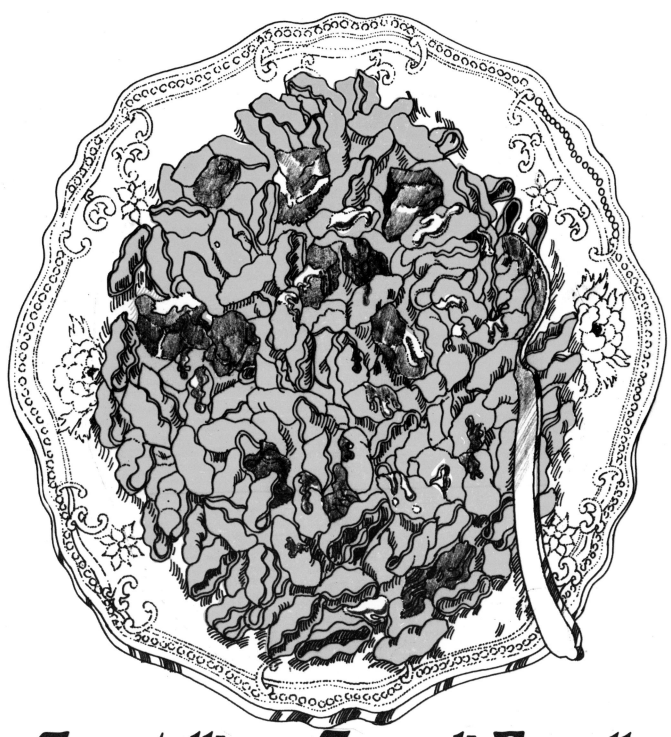

Cavatelli con Sugo di Agnello

Country character is what makes this dish so hearty and delightful.
The succulent pieces of lamb combine extremely well with the rich tomato sauce,
which in turn complements this unusual pasta shape. Great family fare.
(Serves 3–4)

Sauces

Salsa di Pomodoro
(Basic Tomato Sauce)

1 large onion, chopped
2 tablespoons oil
1 clove garlic, chopped (optional)
1 large 2-pound can tomatoes
or 2 pounds fresh tomatoes, peeled and chopped
3 level tablespoons tomato paste
1 teaspoon dried basil
½ teaspoon sugar
salt and pepper to taste

Sauté onion in oil until soft and transparent. Do not let the onion brown. Add the garlic (if used) and sauté one minute. Stir in the tomatoes and juice, breaking them up with a wooden spoon. Add the tomato paste, basil, sugar and a pinch of salt and pepper. Simmer the sauce, partially covered, for 30–40 minutes, until it has reduced to a thick consistency that will coat the back of a spoon. Stir sauce often to prevent burning. Strain it through a fine sieve, pressing down hard on the tomatoes and onions. Add more salt and pepper if needed. This makes about 1 pint of sauce which can be used over any kind of pasta or in baked dishes. It will keep for weeks, tightly covered, in the refrigerator, so you can make many times the quantity and use some when needed.

Ragù di Manzo
(Beef Sauce)

1 large onion, finely chopped
2 tablespoons oil
1–3 cloves garlic, crushed (optional)
1 pound ground beef
one 1-pound can tomatoes
or 1 pound fresh tomatoes, peeled and chopped
2 tablespoons tomato paste
1 teaspoon dried oregano
1 teaspoon dried basil
1 bay leaf
salt and pepper to taste
⅜–½ cup red wine

Sauté onion in oil until soft and transparent. Add garlic and cook another minute. Add ground beef and cook it until brown and crumbly. Break up any lumps with a wooden spoon. Pour off accumulated fat. Stir in tomatoes, breaking them up with a wooden spoon, tomato paste, oregano, basil, bay leaf, and a little salt and pepper. Simmer the sauce, partially covered, stirring often, for 30–40 minutes. Before serving, stir in the wine off the heat. Serve this sauce over any pasta, and serve plenty of grated parmesan with it.

Marinara Sauce

3 tablespoons oil
1 large onion, chopped
1 small carrot, chopped
1–2 cloves garlic, crushed
one 2-pound can tomatoes
or 2 pounds fresh tomatoes, peeled and chopped
1 teaspoon dried oregano
¼ teaspoon dried basil
salt and pepper to taste

Sauté in oil the onion, carrot and garlic for about 5 minutes. Add the tomatoes, breaking them up with a wooden spoon. Add the oregano and basil and simmer, partially covered, for about 30 minutes. Strain sauce through a fine sieve, pushing down hard on the vegetables. Reheat if necessary. If the sauce is too thin, boil it down, uncovered, over a medium heat, until it has reduced to the desired consistency. Season with salt and pepper to taste. This sauce can be served over any kind of pasta.

Ragù Bolognese
(Bolognese Sauce)

3 tablespoons butter
4 slices bacon, chopped
1 large onion, finely chopped
1 medium carrot, finely chopped
1 stalk celery, finely chopped
2 tablespoons oil
⅓ pound ground beef
⅓ pound ground pork
⅓ pound ground veal
½ cup white wine
2 cups beef stock
3 tablespoons tomato paste
1 teaspoon dried oregano
a little grated nutmeg
salt and pepper to taste
1 cup heavy cream (optional)

Melt butter in a frying pan and in it sauté the bacon, onion, carrot and celery. Cook, uncovered, stirring often, for about 10 minutes. Set aside till needed. Heat the oil in another saucepan and in it brown the meats, breaking up any lumps with a wooden spoon, until the mixture is brown and crumbly. Pour off fat, see page 11. Stir in wine over medium high heat letting most of it evaporate. Stir in beef stock, tomato paste, oregano, nutmeg and a little salt and pepper. Add reserved vegetables and bacon. Simmer mixture, partially covered, until it has reduced to a thick sauce, about 40–60 minutes. Add all or some of the cream, if wanted. Don't let it boil again. When served over pasta adding cream rounds off the flavors. But it should not be used in baked dishes incorporating besciamella, such as lasagne, because the dish will lack contrast in color and flavor.

Besciamella
(Bechamel Sauce)

6 tablespoons butter
4 tablespoons flour
2½ cups milk
salt and pepper to taste
a little ground nutmeg

Melt the butter in a saucepan. Make a roux by adding the flour, and stirring with a wire whisk until the flour has been absorbed by the butter. Don't let it brown! Slowly add the milk, stirring quickly and constantly with a wire whisk. Raise the heat, stirring all the time, until the sauce comes to the boil and thickens. Cook, uncovered, still stirring, for 3 minutes. Season with salt, pepper and nutmeg. This sauce is used in many baked pasta dishes.

Pesto alla Genovese
(Genoese Pesto)

1–3 cloves garlic
¾ pint fresh basil leaves (leaves only)
2–3 oz grated parmesan *or* romano cheese
2 tablespoons finely chopped pine nuts
or blanched almonds (optional)
salt and pepper to taste
1¼ cups olive oil

Mash garlic and basil to a smooth paste with a mortar and pestle, or use a bowl and the back of a spoon. Add cheese and nuts, and press them down. Mix in the salt and pepper. Whisk in the oil slowly, in an even stream. The sauce should be very smooth. This sauce can also be made in an electric blender. Blend all ingredients except cheese, at high speed until sauce is smooth and fairly thick. (Push down several times if necessary.) Pour into a bowl. If sauce is too thick, thin down with some oil as required. Blend in the cheese. This sauce can be served over any pasta dish.

INDEX